SADLIER
FAITH AND
WITNESS

LITURGY AND WORSHIP

A Course on Prayer and Sacraments

Rev. Thomas Richstatter, O.F.M., S.T.D.

William H. Sadlier, Inc.
9 Pine Street
New York, New York 10005-1002
http://www.sadlier.com

Acknowledgments

Scripture selections are taken from the *New American Bible* copyright ©1991, 1986, 1970 by the Confraternity of Christian Doctrine, Washington, D.C. and are used by license of the copyright owner. All rights reserved. No part of the *New American Bible* may be used or reproduced in any form without permission in writing from the copyright owner.

Excerpts from the English translation of the *Catechism of the Catholic Church* for use in the United States of America, copyright ©1994, United States Catholic Conference, Inc.—Libreria Editrice Vaticana.

Excerpts from the English translation of *Rite of Marriage* ©1969, International Committee on English in the Liturgy, Inc. (ICEL); excerpts from the English translation of *Rite of Holy Week* ©1972, ICEL; excerpts from the English translation of *The Roman Missal* ©1973, ICEL; excerpts from the English translation of *The Liturgy of the Hours* ©1974, ICEL; excerpts from the English translation of *Rite of Penance* ©1974, ICEL; excerpts from the English translation of *Ordination of Deacons, Priests, and Bishops* ©1975, ICEL; excerpts from the English translation of *Dedication of a Church and an Altar* ©1978, ICEL; excerpts from the English translation of *A Book of Prayers* ©1982, ICEL; excerpts from the English translation of *Documents on the Liturgy, 1963-1979: Conciliar, Curial, and Papal Texts* ©1982, ICEL; excerpts from the English translation of *Rite of Christian Initiation of Adults* ©1986, ICEL; excerpts from the English translation of *Order of Crowning an Image of the Blessed Virgin Mary* ©1986, ICEL. All rights reserved.

The English translation of the Nicene Creed, the Gloria in Excelsis, the Sursum Corda, the Sanctus, the Lord's Prayer, and the Gloria Patri by the International Consultation on English Texts (ICET). All rights reserved.

Excerpt from *Catholic Household Blessings and Prayers* © 1988 United States Catholic Conference, Washington, D.C. Used with permission. All rights reserved.

Excerpt from TURN! TURN! TURN! (To Everything There Is a Season), words from the Book of Ecclesiastes, adaptation and music by Peter Seeger, TRO © Copyright 1962 (renewed) Melody Trails, Inc., New York, N.Y. Used by permission.

Excerpt from AMEN! in the Winter 1995 issue of CHURCH Magazine, published by the National Pastoral life Center,18 Bleecker Street, New York, N.Y. 10012. Used with permission.

Quotation reprinted from JULIAN OF NORWICH: SHOWINGS, translated by Edmund Colledge, O.S.A. and James Walsh, S.J. ©1978 by The Missionary Society of St. Paul the Apostle in the State of New York.

Cover Illustrator: Glynnis Osher
Text Illustrator: Genine Smith: 9, 33, 80, 93, 141, 165

Photo Credits

Jim Saylor
Photo Editor

Lori Berkowitz
Associate Photo Editor

Diane J. Ali: 167 right, 170 left. *Art Resource/* 36 left, 109, 165; Pierpont Morgan Library: 26; Scala: 54–55 right; Foto Marburg 81; Erich Lessing: 116. *Bavaria/ Viesti Asscociates:* 152. *Lori Berkowitz:* 58 right. *Bettmann:* 11 right. *Bridge Building Images/* Robert Lentz: 167 left, 168 left. *Lee Boltin Picture Library:* 47, 50, 162–163, 168 center, 168 right. *Myrleen Cate:* 49, 70, 98 top, 123, 140 left. *Catholic News Service:* 166 left. *Christie's Images:* 26-27. *Karen Callaway:* 144, 145. *Carr Clifton:* 90–91. *Comstock:* 69, 155. *Crosiers/* Gene Plaisted, OSC: 22, 34, 42 right, 44, 45, 46, 51, 59, 60 left, 63, 71 left, 74, 75, 78 right, 79, 82–83, 95, 99, 104, 106 top, 120, 130 left, 131, 134, 146, 156 left, 157, 166 center, 169, 176, 177, 182 left. *FPG International/* Barbara Peacock: 31 center left, 96; D. Dietrich: 54–55 left; C. Franklin: 62–63; Laurance Aiuppi: 96–97; Wayne Levin: 128; Miguel Salmeron: 151; Gerard Loucei: 153; Bill Losh: 154 right; Arthur Tilley: 158. *The Franciscans:* 43 bottom. *Art Glaser:* 84. *The Granger Collection:* 58 left, 58 background; 129, 170 right, 178–179 bottom, 179. *Anne Hamersky:* 20, 27, 42 left, 48, 61 left & center, 71 right, 108, 130 right, 140 right. *Richard & Amy Hutchings:* 159. *Image Bank/* Harald Sund: 14; Siqui Sanchez: 78–79; Anthony A. Buccaccio: 80; Stephen Marks: 111, 156 right; Michael Melford: 164; Terje Rakke: 182 right. *Institute for Our African Ancestors, Inc.:* 166 right. *International Stock:* 110. *St. Joseph's Abbey/* Br. Emmanuel Morinelli, OCSO: 119. *Ken Karp:* 56, 62. *Liaison International/* Livio Anticoli: 138–139. *Greg Lord:* 171. *St. Louise Parish,* Bellevue, WA: 72. *Ron Mamot:* 78 left. *Maryknoll:* 167 center. *Masterfile/* Courtney Milne: 8–9, 10. *Minden Pictures/* Frans Lanting: 6–7. *NASA:* 183. *National Geographic Image Collection/* Raymond Gehman: 126–127. *Our Lady of the Most Holy Rosary Catholic Community in Albuquerque, NM:* 73. *Sarma Ozols:* 92. *Panoramic Images/* Koji Yamashita: 180–181. *Photo Edit/* Michael Newman: 60 right, 61 right. *Photo Researchers, Inc./* World Satellite: 102–103 background. *Photonica/* Mya Kramer: 115; Yasushi Kurada: 150–151; Takeshi Odawara: 122. *Picture Perfect/* Warwick Buddle: 114–115. *Picturesque/* Tom Stamm: 106–107 background. *H. Armstrong Roberts:* 91. *James L. Shaffer:* 48 background, 121, 135. *Nancy Sheehan:* 21, 43 top. *Chris Sheridan:* 37, 39, 94, 98 right, 106 bottom, 107, 132–133, 142, 143. *Jacqueline Srouji:* 87. *The Stock Market/* Joseph Sohm: 66–67. *Superstock:* 24, 32, 154 left. *Sygma/* G. Giansanti: 102–103 foreground. *Tony Stone Images/* Ed Simpson: 11 left; George Grigoriou: 11 center; Gary Holscher: 12 left, 42–43 background; Hugh Sitton: 12 bottom; Gerard Del Vecchio: 12–13; Paul Chesley: 13; Pennie Tweedie: 25; M. Townsend: 28 top left, 29 center right; Ralph Wetmore: 28 top right; David Olsen: 28 center right, 29 bottom left; John Noble: 28 center; Zigy Kaluzny: 174–175; Emmanuelle Dal Secco: 178; William J. Hebert: 184–185. *Uniphoto:* 18–19. *Garth Vaughan:* 177 border, 178–179 top, 181 border. *Westlight/* W. Warren: 68–69. *Bill Wittman:* 36 right, 57, 85, 93, 98 left, 117.

General Consultant
Rev. Joseph A. Komonchak, Ph.D.

Official Theological Consultant
Most Rev. Edward K. Braxton, Ph.D., S.T.D.
Auxiliary Bishop of St. Louis

Publisher
Gerard F. Baumbach, Ed.D.

Editor in Chief
Moya Gullage

Pastoral Consultant
Rev. Msgr. John F. Barry

Scriptural Consultant
Rev. Donald Senior, C.P., Ph.D., S.T.D.

General Editors
Norman F. Josaitis, S.T.D.
Rev. Michael J. Lanning, O.F.M.

Catechetical and Liturgical Consultants
Eleanor Ann Brownell, D.Min.
Joseph F. Sweeney
Helen Hemmer, I.H.M.
Mary Frances Hession
Maureen Sullivan, O.P., Ph.D.
Don Boyd

"The Ad Hoc Committee to Oversee the Use of the Catechism,
National Conference of Catholic Bishops,
has found this catechetical text to be in conformity
with the *Catechism of the Catholic Church.*"

Home Office:
9 Pine Street
New York, NY 10005–1002

ISBN: 8215-5604-5
123456789/987

CHAPTER 1

More Than Meets the Eye

At present we see indistinctly,
as in a mirror,
but then face to face.

1 Corinthians 13:12

A rock, a flower, a fire, a stream,
A touch, a smile, a goodbye, a dream—
Oh, how these are so much more than they seem!

In what ways can things like these be
"much more than they seem"?

The Real World

You are about to enter into a whole new way of looking at life and faith. Now that you are more mature, it is time to go deeper in understanding exactly what Christ meant when he said, "Where two or three are gathered together in my name, there am I in the midst of them" (Matthew 18:20).

Jesus is with us, especially when we gather to celebrate the liturgy. But how does this happen? To begin our challenging exploration, we must get back to basics and start with our human experience of signs and symbols.

Have you ever heard the expression, "There's more here than meets the eye"? It means that often

things can suggest images, emotions, or meanings beyond what we can see with our eyes. When this happens, the things become symbols. A *symbol* is something that stands for or suggests something else. *Symbol* comes from a Greek word that means "to throw together." When something we observe with our senses is "thrown together" with the unseen—a memory, a feeling, or an idea—it can become a symbol.

How does this happen? To answer this question let's take a look at fire. The discovery of fire was an earthshaking moment in human history.

The Power of Symbol

Have you ever watched an award ceremony at the Olympics? What happens? The gold medal is given to the champion because gold is the most precious of all metals. If you have watched, however, you will observe that for most winners having the medal placed around their necks is not the most moving or symbolic moment. It's what comes next that stirs deep feelings. All stand as the flag of the champion's country is raised and its national anthem is played. This moment is so rich in symbolism that no matter who the gold medal winner is, all who watch understand the symbolic meanings behind the sound of the music and the sight of a flag.

Over time and cultures certain things or acts have come to have deeper meanings that are recognized by the people of that culture. There is a kind of "sign language" that uncovers a deeper world of meanings, ideas, and emotions. That sign language is made up of symbols. A multicolored piece of cloth, as we have seen, arouses feelings of patriotism. A dove suggests the human desire for peace.

Among all the creatures of earth, we humans are the only ones who have the power and the imagination to think symbolically, to interpret and make sense of our lives, and to express in symbols our deepest beliefs and concerns. What does all that have to do with our Catholic faith and with this course on liturgy and worship?

You're about to find out. This book will invite you to celebrate your faith in a way you have never done before. It will challenge you to look at things you thought were familiar in a whole new way. Why now? Because you are ready to experience your faith on a deeper and more mature level. Don't be afraid of the challenge. Let's begin!

And down through the centuries the image of fire has become a symbol of great power. Human beings see in fire so much more than simple scientific combustion. Fire has many symbolic meanings: light, energy, safety, warmth, even godlikeness.

We are so accustomed to the reality of fire that perhaps we are not always aware of its symbolism. But have you ever sat beside a campfire or before a fireplace and been fascinated by the flames—their movements, their sound, their warmth, their colors? If you have, you have engaged in symbolic thinking, just as so many others have done down through the ages.

Sacred Space

We can see from the signs that have been left us that ancient peoples used symbols to express their deep beliefs and concerns about the great mysteries of life, concerns that we share today: Who are we? Who made us? Why are we here? Who directs our lives? Does anyone care for us?

This awareness of the divine, the holy, the sacred appears in every human culture. It is expressed differently in different cultures; but in all of them, symbols are part of the way we humans communicate our belief in the sacred. And just as we do today, the ancient peoples set aside symbolic *places* in which to celebrate the sacred mysteries of life.

Consider, for example, Native Americans. They saw no need to build sacred spaces because they believed deeply that the land—all of it—is sacred: every rock, every tree, every river, every canyon. Everything from the smallest insect to the highest mountain is sacred to them because it was placed here by the creator. And because all things are sacred, all places are sacred, too.

Still, Native Americans chose certain special places on the sacred land in which to celebrate their deepest beliefs. In these chosen places they have left us many symbols of their beliefs and concerns: serpent mounds, rock paintings, medicine wheels, rock carvings, and totem poles, among others. At the heart of these symbols is their belief in the relationship human beings have with one another, with the land, and with the Great Spirit, the creator.

At the summit of a mountain in northern Wyoming, there is a great stone wheel or circle impressed on the earth. Spokes radiate from the center of the wheel to its edge. Native Americans believe that the circle symbolizes infinity because it has no beginning and no end. Native peoples of the area have oral histories about the sacred ceremonies held at this symbolic place. Even today prayer offerings are left on the mountain.

 Have you ever been to a place sacred to a culture other than your own? If so, share your experience.

Medicine Mountain, Wyoming

Machu Picchu, Acropolis, Saint Peter's Basilica

Symbols of Belief

Native Americans are not the only ones with sacred places, of course. In every age and culture, the holy place—a shrine, forest grove, temple, church—has been symbolically set apart as a sacred area. The placement of objects in the sacred place symbolizes the belief of the people. Sacred places are often considered to be reflections of the universe. The domes of Christian churches, often painted with stars, are symbols of heaven; the altar, a symbol of Christ. The inner sanctuary in Shinto shrines in Japan is a symbol of God, and the prayer niches in mosques of Islam are symbols of the presence of Allah.

The ancient Greeks saw their highest mountain, Mount Olympus, as the dwelling place of the gods, where they lived shrouded from men's eyes by the mists. The Athenians chose the highest hill in their city as their sacred place. There on the Acropolis (meaning "high city"), they constructed a sacred temple to their gods, especially Athena, the protective goddess of their people.

The remains of Machu Picchu, the sacred city of the Inca, lie at the top of the Andes mountains, symbolically close to the heavens and suggesting symbolically the efforts humans must make to approach the sacred.

As we have seen, expressing our beliefs in symbol is part of our humanity. And one of the most profound symbols of all is that of the space we set apart in which to worship.

What about us? What do our sacred places symbolize? Our sacred places and spaces express our deepest beliefs as Catholics. Our most profound belief is that Jesus Christ, the Son of God, became one of us. He suffered, died, and rose again so that we might have new life. All our sacred places, objects, and actions help us to enter more deeply into this mystery of our salvation through Jesus Christ.

During this course we have the opportunity to look at and to celebrate these beliefs in a new and more mature way, to decide what they mean to us, and to allow them to change our lives.

CATHOLIC ID For us Catholics, all our churches are sacred spaces. Each is the "house of God" because Christ is present there in the Eucharist. Your own parish church is a sacred space. Some places, however, hold deeper significance for us because of their location or because of something that happened there. Saint Peter's Basilica in Vatican City is one such sacred space. From the earliest centuries of the Church, Christians believed that this was the place where Saint Peter was martyred and buried. Excavations beneath Saint Peter's have uncovered a *necropolis*, a "city of the dead." Inscriptions and bones found there seem to confirm that this is indeed the burial place of Saint Peter.

Symbols in Action

It is 1963. An assassinated president is being laid to rest. President Kennedy's flag-draped coffin is brought from the cathedral and placed on a horse-drawn gun carriage for the procession to Arlington National Cemetery. Behind the gun carriage a soldier leads a riderless horse. There is no music for this procession, only the sound of muffled drums and the creaking of the carriage wheels.

At the cemetery members of the military fold the flag, with solemn precision, into an intricate and prescribed triangle and present it to the widow. Three buglers play in echoing sequence the plaintive *Taps,* the sound that ends a soldier's day. Mrs. Kennedy then lights an "eternal flame," a light that will never go out, on the president's grave.

This event, indelibly imprinted on the memories of those who witnessed it, is rich in symbols. How many can you discover?

When symbols are connected like this in meaningful action, we have what is called a ritual. *Rituals,* then, are symbolic actions that often express our deepest beliefs or concerns. Some rituals, of course, are very simple, such as placing candles on a birthday cake, doing the wave at a baseball game, or giving a teammate a high five after a victory.

Other rituals, such as the funeral described above, the opening ceremonies of the Olympic Games, or a graduation ceremony, have deeper and more complicated symbolism.

Recall a wedding that you have attended or seen. Describe some of its symbolic ritual. In what way does the ritual express deeper meanings and beliefs?

These pictures show people of other faiths expressing their beliefs in rituals. How do we express our Catholic beliefs?

What Makes a Ritual?

Anthropologists tell us that rituals, or symbolic actions, are at the heart of human experience. From earliest times human beings have developed rituals to celebrate, remember, and express in a public way their deepest concerns, their most profound beliefs. Rituals are found among human beings in every age and from every culture, from the cave paintings of prehistoric humans to the Eucharist celebrated today in our parish churches. Somehow rituals meet deep human needs of individuals and communities. They often mark transitions from one stage of life to another. They help us make sense of life's mysteries.

What are some characteristics of ritual? Here are three of the most important ones.

• Ritual is *interpersonal*. It is something one does not alone but with others who share the same beliefs or concerns. When symbolic action is expressed by people as a community, its deepest meanings are revealed and experienced.

• Ritual is *repetitive*. Humans repeat rituals because these actions express what is most constant, most meaningful in their lives. We celebrate ritually what is unchanging to us in a changing world. If an action is true and meaningful to us, it must be repeated, celebrated, over and over again.

• Ritual is *acted out*. It uses symbolic movements and gestures to express deeper meaning. These actions are symbolic because they go beyond what is seen on the surface.

For example, do you know why the ritual of greeting someone by shaking hands arose? What to us is now an automatic action of greeting was once a very serious and very symbolic action. In the early Middle Ages, it was a sign to strangers or possible foes that one was not holding a weapon and therefore was not a threat to the other. Once men shook hands, both were committed by honor to obey its meaning and not to attack one another during their meeting. The symbol persisted into later ages, when a man's handshake was equivalent to his word. "Let's shake on it" came into the language of business and diplomacy as a symbol of one's word of honor.

An understanding of symbol and ritual is essential to a mature understanding of our worship as Catholics. All the sacraments of the Church involve ritual. And if we are aware and willing to participate, each ritual draws us more deeply into the life of faith it expresses.

Scripture UPDATE

One beautiful way to look at symbols in Scripture is found in the story of the prodigal son (Luke 15:11–32). Remember when the younger son came home? His father *ran* to meet him. He *hugged* and *kissed* his son even before saying a word. What clearer symbols could the son have had of his father's love?

What does this picture symbolize to you?

Thinking Symbolically

In this chapter we have explored symbols: objects, places, and actions that have meanings beyond what we can perceive with our physical senses alone. All people of a given culture recognize and identify with these meanings. Of course a person has to have had some cultural experiences and a certain maturity to be aware of symbolic meanings. You are certainly ready to begin to think symbolically.

See if you can recognize the meanings of these symbols. If you are not sure, use your imagination. See how close you can come to the universal understanding of each one.

Symbol	Meaning
At the coronation of Elizabeth II, the young queen was given symbolic objects: a scepter and a golden orb (a sphere). What do these stand for?	
A bishop carries a shepherd's staff. It is called a *crosier*. Why a shepherd's staff?	
A traditional symbol of justice is a statue of a woman. She wears a blindfold and holds balanced scales in her hands. What do these symbols say about justice?	
A Chinese proverb says, "It is better to light one candle than to curse the darkness." How are these words symbolic?	

Share your ideas. See how aware you already are of complex symbolism.

 Can you describe some other symbols that are universally recognized?

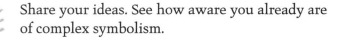

Ritual Celebrations

Like symbols, rituals, such as a salute or a handshake, can be very simple. They can also be much more complex, much richer, especially those dealing with people's cultural memories and deepest beliefs.

In the spaces here describe the rituals that are celebrated on each occasion. To the general rituals that most people celebrate, add any further details that are a part of your family's rituals.

We have spent a great deal of time on symbol and ritual in this opening chapter. Why? Because symbolic thinking is one of the most essential and profound things humans can do. Symbolic thinking is certainly the most essential and profound thing we do as Catholics. And when we grow in appreciating and understanding the symbols and rituals of our faith, they will speak to us as nothing else in the world does.

This will take hard work and effort. But by the time we finish this course, we will see with new eyes the power and effect of what we do together as Catholics. As we will see, the Church takes elements from creation and from our human activity and sanctifies them—makes them holy— and enables them to be signs of grace.

CATHOLIC TEACHINGS

About Sacramental Signs

The Church's sacramental celebrations involve not only signs and symbols relating to creation and human life but also to God's mighty deeds for his people, above all the Passover. Through the power of the Holy Spirit, these signs and symbols become "bearers of the saving and sanctifying action of Christ" (*Catechism*, 1189).

Thanksgiving

Christmas

Fourth of July

things
to think about

Name some simple human rituals. Describe a more complex human ritual.

Make an imaginary or real visit to your parish church. Name the religious symbols you see.

things
to share

Explain this statement: Symbols can affect our memories and our emotions.

Why is an understanding of religious symbols and rituals essential to a mature understanding of Catholic worship?

WORDS TO REMEMBER

Find and define the following:

symbol _____

_____

_____

ritual _____

_____

_____

OnLine
WITH THE PARISH

Singing is a vital and vocal way to participate in the prayer of the Church. As a group talk about ways you might encourage yourselves and other young people to join in praising God in song. Perhaps the parish choir director would be willing to help you. This might also be one important way you can prepare for a Mass together later in this course.

Choose a symbol that is part of your culture. Describe how this object affects you on a deeper level.

1

What does the word *symbol* come from? What does this word root tell you about the way a symbol works?

2

List and explain three characteristics of ritual.

3

Why are sacred places important in some rituals?

4

Why are symbol and ritual essential to us?

5

Life
in the Spirit

Simple symbols can often help us to develop our personal prayer life. Here are a few ideas:

When you need help or strength, find a rock that fits in the palm of your hand. Hold it and feel it as you pray, "Jesus, you are the rock of my hope. You are my refuge and my strength."

Find a shell, fill it with water, and then slowly let the water flow out. Pray, "Jesus help me to empty from my life all things that keep it from being filled with you."

Hold a leaf in your hand. Look at it as closely as you can. See its intricacy and beauty. Thank God for the wonders of his creation.

CHAPTER 2

The Prayer
of the Church

Lord, teach us to pray.

Luke 11:1

In every culture human beings express their beliefs and hopes in symbolic ways. Think of the ways that we as Catholics express our hopes and beliefs.

Catholic Symbols and Rituals

Words alone can never fully express the deep meanings of our Catholic faith. Because we are human beings, because we have bodies and live in the world of created things, we often use symbols to express our thoughts and feelings, our understandings and insights. As we have seen, a symbol is an object or action that stands for something else. For example, people in love not only talk about loving each other; they also

exchange gifts. That is, they give symbols of their love. In the same way, when we celebrate our love relationship with God, we do so not only with words but also with objects and gestures. These are symbols, too.

When we Catholics pray together, we celebrate in and through *symbolic* activity. We must use the language of symbol in our prayer because we are discovering and celebrating what is invisible to our eyes. Remember that signs and symbols put us in touch with what we cannot see. Catholic worship is filled with symbols: eating and drinking, being plunged into water and anointed with oil, standing and sitting, processing from place to place, raising our hands, speaking out and singing together. As Catholics we must never forget that these signs and symbols of our faith put us in touch with the divine. Through them we share in God's own divine life.

The church, the sacred place where we meet for worship, is full of symbols: light, fire, water, word, incense. Often the very architecture of a church is symbolic. Many of our churches are cross-shaped in design, a symbol of our redemption. Others are circular, symbolic of the public nature of our worship.

We use the things of this earth in our prayer because we believe that creation is good. By using created things, we worship the God of creation, the God who "looked at everything he had made, and he found it very good" (Genesis 1:31).

The prayer of the Church is not only *symbolic* activity; it is also *ritual* activity. Rituals are actions we do over and over in prescribed, formal, and set ways. In our daily lives we carry out many ritual actions. Can you think of some ordinary things we do ritually each day?

The prayer of the Church, too, is expressed in rituals. We do things over and over in prescribed, formal, and set ways. Rituals are characteristic of Catholic worship. It would be obvious to a visitor attending Mass for the first time that Catholics know the rituals and are comfortable with them. Catholics know "what happens next," what to expect. When the priest greets us with, "The Lord be with you," we respond, without any thought or hesitation, "And also with you." When the priest invites us, "Let us pray," we stand up. Our rituals help us to do together what we came to do: celebrate Christ's saving actions in our lives.

We Catholics perform many ritual actions during our liturgical celebrations. Perhaps you have never thought about the meaning of these rituals. But understanding what is being said and done through ritual helps us to participate in the prayer of the Church. This is true of anything we do. Isn't it true that the activities which we find boring are often the ones which we do not understand?

The same is true of the prayer of the Church. We can't participate well if we don't understand its symbols and rituals. In order to pray well and to come to know what that prayer means in daily life, it is important for us to acquire the skills and understanding that are necessary to celebrate the prayer of the Church with enthusiasm and joy.

In this course we will discover how Catholics have traditionally prayed and worshiped God. We will explore the liturgy and the sacraments, the Church year, and Catholic devotions. We will learn about the rituals and ceremonies that Catholics have used through the centuries to become God's friends. In this way we, too, can come to know how much we are loved by God. Through that knowledge we will come to appreciate even more what it means to be a Catholic.

A deacon accepting the offerings of bread and wine at the preparation of the gifts

The Prayer of the Church

Liturgy is the public prayer of the Church in which we proclaim and celebrate the mystery of Christ. Originally the word *liturgy* meant "a public work"— literally, a work for the people, for everyone.

Because the public prayer of the Church is for everyone, it came to be called *liturgy,* which now means "the participation of the people in the work of God." What is the work of God? It is the work of our redemption; it is what Christ did for us. Liturgy is a work by and for the people, but above all it is God's work. In liturgy the mission of Christ—the work of his passion, death, resurrection, and ascension—continues today.

Liturgical prayer, as God's work and the work of the people, the Church, is a very particular kind of prayer. What are some of its characteristics?

Public First, as we have already seen, liturgical prayer is *public* prayer. Yet it is public in a very special way. Not all prayers said in public are liturgical. For example, a group of people may gather in church to say the rosary. Or perhaps you have seen pictures of the Holy Father on Good Friday leading the stations of the cross in the Coliseum in Rome. Hundreds of people participate. These are certainly public acts, but liturgical prayer is public in a deeper sense.

Liturgical prayer is public because each liturgical celebration, such as the Mass or the sacraments, includes, concerns, and affects the whole Church community. It is the official prayer of the Church. And because liturgical prayer is always for the entire Church, it is public even when only a small number of people are present.

Prayer of Christ Liturgical prayer is the prayer of Christ himself. Because it is the prayer of Christ, liturgical prayer has unique and special value above and beyond anything else we, as Church, could possibly do.

Worship of the Trinity Liturgical prayer is always prayer to the Blessed Trinity. Every liturgical celebration is offered in, with, and through *Jesus Christ*, in the unity of the *Holy Spirit*, to the honor and glory of the *Father*. Liturgical prayer is always worship of the Trinity.

Addressed to God Liturgical prayer is always addressed to God. Even when we honor Mary and the other saints in the liturgy, we praise and thank God for them. In our private prayer we are always free to call on Mary and the saints directly. In the liturgy, however, our focus is God. In our private prayer we can ask God for all sorts of things. In liturgical prayer, because it is the voice of Christ, we pray for those things that Christ wants. What things do you think Christ wants?

In the Words of the Church In our private prayer we are free to use whatever words we choose. We are encouraged to pray freely and spontaneously, both alone and sometimes with others. In liturgical prayer, however, we pray in the words and with the actions given to us by the Church. Words and actions, carefully preserved and treasured for centuries, are handed down to us in the rites and rituals given in liturgical books.

You may already be familiar with a few of these liturgical books. One, the large book that you see the priest use at the altar during Mass, is the sacramentary. It contains the prayers for the Eucharist. Another book you might know is the lectionary. The name comes from *lectio,* the Latin word for "reading." This is the book that the reader, or lector, carries in procession at the beginning of the Eucharist and from which the Scriptures are proclaimed.

Communal and Personal

Liturgy is the public prayer of the Church in worship of the Trinity. In the liturgy we pray with Christ, the head of the Church, and with his whole body, the Church on earth and in heaven. Now that's public!

Do you think it is possible to be both *public* and *personal* at the same time? Have you ever been with a group of people celebrating a victory, a memorial, or another special moment in life? You are all experiencing something together, but at the same time you are feeling it personally, individually.

That is what liturgy is like. It is a communal experience and a personal experience at the same time. Good liturgy is never private, but good liturgy is always personal.

Liturgical prayer is the prayer of Christ. What do you think might be some of the concerns of Christ that are expressed in the liturgy? Which of those concerns are yours as well?

CATHOLIC TEACHINGS

About Liturgy

The liturgy is the most important activity of the Church because it is the work of Christ himself. However, liturgy can never be the *only* activity of the Church. We must believe the good news and live as Jesus' disciples. This means we "love and serve the Lord" by loving and serving others. Liturgy sends us out to serve others, and that experience sends us back to celebrate liturgy. Liturgy and loving service form one unbroken circle.

The Crucifixion, Georges Rouault, 1939

From Death to Life

There is an ancient saying in the Church: "The way we pray shows what we believe." The liturgy, the public prayer of the Church, is the official way we pray as Catholics. In what way does the prayer of the Church show what we believe?

What makes us who we are as Catholics is our relationship to the Father in and through Jesus Christ. We believe in Jesus Christ—in who he is and in what God has accomplished in him. What makes us Catholic is our belief in the paschal mystery of Jesus.

What is the paschal mystery of Jesus Christ? By the *paschal mystery* we mean all that God has done to redeem us in Christ Jesus, especially in his suffering, death, resurrection, and ascension. We proclaim this paschal mystery at every Eucharist when we say:

Dying you destroyed our death,
rising you restored our life.
Lord Jesus, come in glory.

Christ has died, Christ is risen, Christ will
come again.

The word *paschal* refers to Passover, the feast of freedom for the people of Israel. During this great feast, the Jewish people celebrate their deliverance, their passing over, from slavery to freedom. During Holy Week and Easter, we Christians celebrate the "passing over" of Jesus from death to new life. As the liturgy tells us, Jesus Christ is now and always "our Passover and our lasting peace."

Mystery means more than just something that cannot be fully understood. It also means *a truth that continually calls us to deeper understanding,* a truth so wonderful that we are continually drawn to investigate the depths of its meaning.

To discover what the paschal mystery really means is the work of a lifetime. Catholics believe that the birth, life, suffering, death, resurrection, and ascension of Jesus Christ is the very center of all that exists. When Jesus, in his paschal mystery, passed from death to life, all of creation was made new—including ourselves. His new life is now our new life. It is the central vocation of every Christian to discover and live the meaning of Christ's passion, death, and resurrection in today's world. How do we do this?

Scripture UPDATE

The liturgy of the Church has adopted many Jewish liturgical symbols and rituals. Many of these are mentioned in Scripture: praying the psalms as responses; using musical instruments and incense in worship; setting aside one day a week, the Sabbath, as a day of rest and prayer. Among the most important of these practices that we still observe is the reading of the Old Testament in our liturgy. This practice is "irreplaceable" (*Catechism,* 1093).

Living the Paschal Mystery

The first step is to begin to develop a personal relationship with God, for it is our *person* that we bring to the public prayer of the Church. We do not come to the celebration of Christ's paschal mystery as strangers in God's presence or even as mere acquaintances. We come as Jesus' own friends and disciples, just as his first followers did.

Usually friendship does not just happen. We have to work at a relationship. We have to spend time with the other person. We have to develop common interests. We have to want what is good for the other, and we need to be willing to sacrifice for the other.

We become friends with God in much the same way, spending time with him, developing common interests, learning about God, sharing our concerns, our dreams, our hopes. That is what praying really is.

And even though we may not realize it, God is waiting for us to come to him. God, after all, tops the list of those who love us. He sees, knows, and loves us as we really are. God shows his love for us through Jesus Christ and through the Church. And it is in praying with the Church "through Jesus Christ, our Lord" that we come to recognize and respond to him in a personal way.

If some people find the liturgy long or dull or boring, it may be because they have not yet grown up enough to establish a real relationship, a friendship with God.

As Saint Gregory of Nyssa, a fourth-century bishop, said, "The one thing worthwhile is becoming God's friend."

What is your relationship with God like? Do you work at it? How? Do you come to celebrate liturgy as a stranger, as an acquaintance, or as a friend?

HOMI=
NES HAC LEGE
SVNT GENERATI,
QVI TVERENTVR
ILLVM GLOBVM,
QVEM IN HOC TEM=
PLO MEDIVM VI=
DES, QVAE TER=
RA DICITVR.
Cicero.

SEPTEMTRIO.

TERRA SEPT EMTRIONALIS INCOGNITA.

CIRCVLVS ARCTICVS.

A Little History

A great part of understanding something is knowing where it comes from, its history. Most of us probably enjoy looking through family albums or other family mementos. These things tell us something about the lives of our parents and grandparents. They are part of our family history, a history that shapes our lives.

How did liturgy come to be the way it is today? Our liturgical family has a history, too, a history that has helped to shape our Catholic life. It is a rich and interesting history formed by many languages, many cultures, and many historical events.

What are the roots of our liturgical life? Where do these symbols and rituals come from? We begin with Jesus himself. As we shall see, it is really Jesus who gives us the sacraments and entrusts them to the Church.

When the Son of God became one of us, he did so in a particular culture: Jesus was a Jew who lived in first-century Palestine. His first followers were also Jews. They prayed as Jews. After the resurrection and ascension of Jesus, they continued to pray in the Temple in Jerusalem on the Sabbath. But now they did something new as well.

We read that "every day they devoted themselves to meeting together in the temple area and to breaking bread in their homes" (Acts 2:46). In the Temple they listened to readings from the Old Testament and responded with psalms and prayers. In their homes they shared the Eucharist, as Jesus had instructed them. Even at this early date, we can trace the origin of the two parts of the Mass as we know them today: the Liturgy of the Word and the Liturgy of the Eucharist.

As the good news of Jesus spread from Palestine to Syria, Greece, Africa, and the ends of the Roman Empire, the message was translated into new languages and planted in new cultures. Greek was the common language spoken at that time, so the gospels and the letters of Saint Paul were written in Greek. Later, when Latin became the official language of the Roman Empire, both the Bible and the liturgy were translated into Latin. For many centuries the Latin language served as the principal means for understanding and explaining our faith. It is still used as the official language of the Church in important documents, such as papal encyclicals.

HOC
EST PVNCTVM,
QVOD INTER TOT
GENTES FERRO
ET IGNI DIVIDI=
VR, O QVAM RIDI=
CVLI SVNT MOR=
TALIVM TER=
MINI?
Seneca.

QVID EI POTEST VIDERI MAGNVM IN REBVS HVMA
NITAS OMNIS, TOTIVSQVE MVNDI NOTA SIT MAGNI

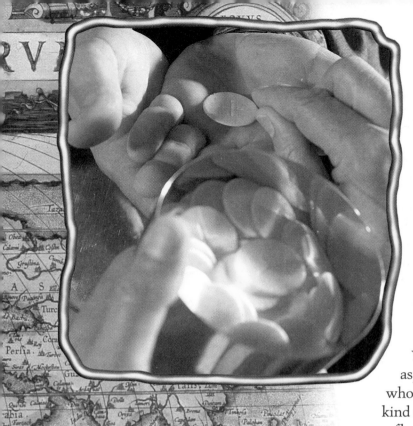

The Liturgy Today

In what ways do we still celebrate the liturgy as the early Christians did? How are we different?

We no longer go to the temple for prayer; instead we go to our parish churches. But we still read the same readings and pray the same psalms as the first Christians did. We no longer read the Scriptures in Latin, as the Romans did; now we read them in our own language. We celebrate the same breaking of the bread, the same Eucharist. The most important parts of the liturgy have not changed. They have been given to us just as they were given to the first followers of Jesus.

Yet our culture today does influence some aspects of liturgy because our culture expresses who we are and what we believe. For example, the kind of music we play and sing at the liturgy is a reflection of our culture. Various instruments are used in church music: pipe organ, guitars, drums, violins, and flutes. The music can range from the quiet reflection of chant to the exuberance of a mariachi band.

The question of change—of what should or should not be changed based on changing culture—is always a very important and serious question for the Church. It is the Church that teaches and guides us in what can be changed and what can never be changed. For example, for two thousand years we have celebrated the Eucharist as the memorial of Christ's death and resurrection. Through sacramental signs we share in this mystery of faith. Bread and wine are transformed into the Body and Blood of Christ. This will never change. The words of institution will never change. How wonderful it is that the Church guides us to this truth and will do so for all time.

CATHOLIC ID

The liturgy is a major part of the tradition of the Church. The word *tradition* means "what is handed down." Because the liturgy is handed down to us from the earliest days of the Church, we look to the teaching authority of the Church to guide our liturgical celebration.

But the liturgy is also flexible and open to various cultures. Can you discover unique cultural expressions in African liturgical worship? Latin American? Asian? Magazines from missionary societies may help you with your search.

"The way we pray shows what we believe." Give one example from the liturgy that shows what we believe as Catholics.

things to think about

What comes to your mind when you say to yourself or someone else, "I'm Catholic"? Think about the words, feelings, or images the word *Catholic* has for you. Brainstorm with your group. Do these ideas have anything to do with prayer or liturgy? Where does Jesus fit in?

things to share

Do you think that you would live any differently if you did not believe in Jesus? Try to imagine how your life would be different if you were not a Catholic. Discuss this with several of your friends.

WORDS TO REMEMBER

Find and define the following:

liturgy _____
_____
_____

paschal mystery _____
_____
_____

OnLine WITH THE PARISH

The Church is universal, welcoming all peoples and cultures. It might be interesting to discover in your parish or diocese how differing cultural expressions in language, music, and other ways to celebrate are encouraged in the liturgy. One way to experience this might be to join in a liturgy celebrated in a language other than your own. Share your reactions with your group.

"The way we pray shows what we believe." Explain.

1

What does the word *liturgy* mean? Name five characteristics of liturgical prayer.

2

What does the word *mystery* mean?

3

What difference does the paschal mystery of Jesus Christ make in our lives?

4

Give an example of how our contemporary culture is expressed in the liturgy.

5

Life in the Spirit

In personal, private prayer we can say anything we want to God. We can pray anytime, anywhere, for any amount of time. Simply thinking quiet, grateful thoughts about God or saying the holy name of Jesus quietly to yourself is prayer. Praying alone is good preparation for liturgical prayer because private prayer also helps us to become aware of the presence of Christ in our lives.

Symbols used in the liturgy can help us focus when we pray privately. Candles, pictures, incense, music—these are symbols that can remind us of God's presence. Which ones do you find helpful?

God's Masterpieces

How great are your works, LORD!

Psalm 92:6

Jesus as the Comforter, August Jerndorff, 1846–1906

Is a sacrament something we pray?
something we do? something we receive or
something we watch? or something else?
What do you think a sacrament is?

God's Master Plan

What is a sacrament? To answer this question, we should start at the very beginning. At the very beginning, when God created the world and everything in it, he had a plan. He didn't start one day and make sky, then make earth, then make light, and then make darkness. He did not continue to create one thing after another without knowing from the very beginning what it would be when it was all finished. The Father had a plan in mind.

Throughout the Old Testament we read about God's plan. Little by little the plan is revealed in the history of his chosen people and through his prophets and messengers. And when the right moment came, this plan was revealed in all its wonderful mystery in the birth, life, passion, death, and resurrection of Jesus Christ. The plan God had in mind was Jesus Christ! In Jesus, God would reveal himself to us most fully. In Jesus, we see God made visible, at once truly human and truly divine.

Jesus, the Word Made Flesh

On page after page of Sacred Scripture, we read of God's mysterious plan. At the very beginning of the Bible, we see God creating this magnificent universe and all that is in it. He creates the world. Then, from the earth, he creates an "earthling," a human person, breathing into it his own image. And all is at peace.

In these first chapters of the Book of Genesis, we glimpse the harmony God plans for the world:

• Men and women are at peace *with each other*: They are partners and helpers to each other.

• The human creatures are at peace *with the earth*: Adam names the animals. He tills the earth, and it brings forth fruit.

• These human creatures are at peace *with God*: Adam walks and talks with him in the garden.

And it is good. This is God's plan: He wants all creation to be reconciled and at peace.

Then sin shatters every layer of the dream. Peace between human beings dissolves; peace with the earth becomes toil and struggle. And peace with God? When God calls to Adam, Adam hides. He no longer walks and talks freely with God. This is the first sin—the *original* sin. And all of us share in its effects: weakness of will, tendency to sin, suffering, and death.

But God did not give up on the plan. When the time was ripe, God sent his only Son to bring it to fulfillment. This is Jesus, the Word made flesh. Jesus spent his life showing us how to be at peace with one another, with creation, and with his Father and ours. He spent his life teaching love and forgiveness, healing sickness and division. His resurrection and ascension was his victory over death and sin. Jesus is our redeemer. Through him we are saved from sin. His sacrifice on the cross and his victory over sin and death made the Father's plan of peace and harmony possible for us and for our world. The paschal mystery is the promise that God's plan will be fulfilled.

 Think for a moment. How are you at peace with others, with creation, and with God? How can you deepen and strengthen this peace?

The Son of God, the second Person of the Blessed Trinity, became one of us in Jesus. In Jesus the invisible God becomes visible! In Jesus we see and come to know the invisible God, whom no eye has ever seen.

This understanding of Jesus is expressed clearly and beautifully in a prayer from the Mass at Christmas. It proclaims that in Jesus,

> we see our God made visible
> and so are caught up in love of the God we
>   cannot see.

The Sacraments

If we ever wonder what God is like, all we have to do is look at Jesus of Nazareth—at what he did, what he said, what he was.

The plan of God did not end with the birth of Jesus. It did not even end with the death of Jesus. For even after death, Jesus carried out God's plan. How? After his resurrection, the risen Christ appeared to his apostles and said, "Receive the holy Spirit" (John 20:22). In handing over the Spirit, Jesus handed over to his descendants— his followers, the Church—his very own life.

This life of Jesus, this Spirit, dwells now in the Church, in us. The invisible life of God, first made visible in Jesus Christ, is now made visible in the Church. And Jesus has given the Church seven special signs to draw us into union with him and the Father through the power of the Spirit. Through the sacraments we encounter Christ. Through the sacraments we share in the saving work of Jesus Christ our redeemer.

A *sign* is something that points the way. Sacraments are signs but they are unique signs. They are signs unlike any other signs in the world. This is because they do more than point the way. They *are* the way. For example, the water of Baptism is not only a sign of life. Through these waters of Baptism, we receive life. In the Eucharist the bread and wine are not only signs of the Body and Blood of Christ. They become the Body and Blood of Christ.

A sacrament actually brings about—that is, makes real and present—what it signifies. When we celebrate the sacraments, we do not simply celebrate salvation, forgiveness, and union with God. We are in fact saved, forgiven, and made one with Jesus Christ. A *sacrament* is a visible and effective sign, given to us by Christ, through which we share in God's grace. No wonder that the Church calls the sacraments "God's masterpieces" (*Catechism*, 1091).

Celebrating the Sacraments

The Church celebrates the seven sacraments. Rejoicing in that faith we received from the apostles, we understand the purpose of the sacraments: to sanctify us, to build up the Church, and to give praise and worship to God. Through the sacraments, our faith is nourished and made strong.

In the celebration of each sacrament, four essential qualities are always present.

Ritual Action A sacrament is God's life in us— grace—expressed in ritual action. Each sacrament has its own symbols and gestures, its own ritual way of expressing the gift of grace being shared. For example, in the sacrament of the Anointing of the Sick, the sick person is anointed with oil in the sign of the cross. The oil and the cross are signs of the healing given by Christ.

Worship of God The sacraments are liturgical prayer, public prayer, and their focus is God. In every sacrament we praise and worship the Holy Trinity in public liturgical prayer.

Paschal Mystery In every sacrament we remember and enter into the paschal mystery. In every sacrament we ourselves are made part of the paschal mystery in a deeper way.

The Power of the Holy Spirit The sacraments are not magic or wishful thinking. They make the paschal mystery present and effective by the power of the Holy Spirit—by what God does.

 Are sacraments something we only receive? How would you answer this, knowing what you know?

 Because the sacraments are so important, the Church reminds us that the sacramental rites cannot be changed by anyone. Even the supreme authority in the Church can only change the liturgy after faithful reflection and "with religious respect for the mystery of the liturgy" (*Catechism*, 1125).

God's Plan in Writing

God wanted the story of his plan to last through the centuries and to have meaning for all peoples. Eventually, from the Book of Genesis in the Old Testament to the Book of Revelation in the New Testament, God's plan was put into writing under the inspiration of the Holy Spirit. This written story of God's plan is what we now call Sacred Scripture.

Each of the seven sacraments celebrates some aspect of the plan of God that has come to fulfillment in Christ and in the Church. Sacred Scripture is the written record of this divine plan as it unfolds in history. But it is more than a history. Sacred Scripture, we know, is the inspired word of God. When it is proclaimed, God is speaking to us. When Catholics celebrate the liturgy, they hear the word of God.

The proclamation of Sacred Scripture plays a prominent role in every liturgical celebration. In every liturgy we read aloud some part of the story of God's plan. Through the Scriptures we are continually reminded of what God has done for us and what God still plans to do—with our cooperation. We listen to the Scripture story to keep alive our faith in God's plan, God's dream for unity and reconciliation: "Thus faith comes from what is heard, and what is heard comes through the word of Christ" (Romans 10:17).

When we celebrate the liturgy and the sacraments, we celebrate God's plan and our Christian story, which is part of that plan. We need the word of God in the Scriptures to help us to hear our story with faith and understanding and to urge us on to complete the work of Christ in the world. That is why we can say that Catholics are truly people of word and sacrament.

Scripture in Liturgy

Let us look more closely at the ways the Scriptures are used in our liturgical celebrations.

• The readings given are from Scripture and are explained in the homily. The psalms, too, are from Scripture.

• The prayers and liturgical songs are drawn from Scripture.

• The symbols and rituals in the liturgy take their meaning from Scripture.

In recent times the Church expanded the amount and the variety of the Scripture readings to be proclaimed. These readings are found in an official liturgical book called the *lectionary*. The *lectionary* contains the Scripture readings assigned to the various days of the Church year. It provides us with a great variety of Scripture readings all through the year. Because it contains the word of God, we treat the lectionary with great respect.

If possible, borrow a lectionary or a missalette from your parish church. Find and read the Scripture readings for Christmas, Easter, or perhaps the feast days of your favorite saints.

As Catholics living in this sin-torn world divided by war and greed, we must continually retell the story of God's plan for unity and reconciliation. We must keep God's dream alive among us. We do this most significantly in the celebration of the liturgy and the sacraments. The sacraments are the celebration of our Catholic story. Sacraments are worded signs. Scripture is the word, the word that gives the sacramental sign its meaning.

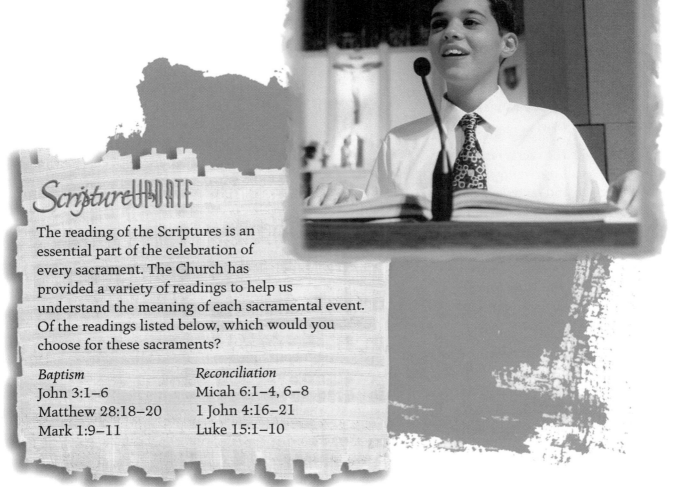

Scripture UPDATE

The reading of the Scriptures is an essential part of the celebration of every sacrament. The Church has provided a variety of readings to help us understand the meaning of each sacramental event. Of the readings listed below, which would you choose for these sacraments?

Baptism
John 3:1–6
Matthew 28:18–20
Mark 1:9–11

Reconciliation
Micah 6:1–4, 6–8
1 John 4:16–21
Luke 15:1–10

In Every Liturgy

The liturgy of the Church has been influenced by many cultures and many languages. We use important words rooted in Hebrew, Greek, and Latin to explain the meaning behind the rituals and symbols of our liturgy. Some of these important words common to every sacrament are *anamnesis, presence, doxology, epiclesis,* and *berakah.* At first these terms may seem strange. But after we are introduced to them and we see how they function in each of the sacraments, they will begin to seem like old friends.

Remembering As we have already seen, recalling and celebrating the paschal mystery is at the heart of liturgical prayer. The term for this "remembering" is *anamnesis.* This word from the Greek means "memory," as in, "Do this in memory [*anamnesis*] of me." *Anamnesis* is the liturgical act of remembering. This special kind of remembering not only calls to mind a saving act of God that happened in the past but also makes that event present to us now.

When we celebrate the sacraments, we are not merely recalling events that happened long ago and far away. We are celebrating events that are present to us now. What began in the past, in the death and resurrection of Jesus, is continued into the present. *Now* Jesus Christ is risen. *Now* the Holy Spirit comes upon us. And *now* we are sent forth by Christ to love and serve.

Presence Christ is always present. The word *presence* comes almost directly from Latin, and means "to be before one"—that is, to be here. The real presence of Christ in the Eucharist has always been at the heart of our Catholic belief. Yet the risen Christ is present and active with us here in each and every sacrament and in every liturgy.

- He is present in the Mass under the signs of bread and wine and in the person of the priest.
- He is present in his power in the sacraments. When a person baptizes, it is really Christ who baptizes.
- He is present in his word when the Scripture is read.
- He is present in the assembly, the community. Jesus himself said, "Where two or three are gathered together in my name, there am I in the midst of them" (Matthew 18:20).

Glory Whenever we recall and make present God's plan for us, we experience feelings of thanksgiving and praise, and we give God glory. Each sacrament and liturgical action is a *doxology,* a prayer that gives God glory. In a more narrow sense, two prayers in particular have been given the title *doxology.* One of these is the Glory to God, the prayer of praise that we sing or recite at the beginning of the Eucharist. Another doxology is "Glory to the Father, and to the Son, and to the Holy Spirit," said at the end of each psalm.

Calling Upon the Holy Spirit In each sacrament we call upon the Spirit to make us holy and to build up the body of Christ. The technical term for this petition is *epiclesis.* Although the words may vary, at each Eucharist we ask God:

Let your Spirit come upon these gifts to make them holy,
so that they may become for us
the body † and blood of our Lord, Jesus Christ.

As we study each of the seven sacraments, look for this prayer of petition, the epiclesis, and see what the prayer asks for. The epiclesis is often the key to understanding the meaning of a sacrament.

THROUGH HIM WITH HIM IN HIM

Blessing One of the prayer forms familiar to Jesus and available to the early Church was the berakah. The *berakah* is not a specific prayer; rather, it is a prayer *form*. The berakah, or prayer of blessing, usually involves three elements: We call on the name of God (invocation). We gratefully remember (anamnesis) all that God has done for us. We make our petition (epiclesis).

Here is an example:

> Blessed are you, Lord, God of all creation.
> Through your goodness we have this bread
> to offer,
> which earth has given and human hands
> have made.
> It will become for us the bread of life.

This last sentence is really a prayer of petition meaning, "God, make it become for us the bread of life."

 In the prayer above indicate the invocation, anamnesis, and epiclesis.

CATHOLIC TEACHINGS

About the Sacraments

The whole liturgical life of the Church revolves around the Eucharist and the other sacraments. There are seven sacraments:

- Baptism
- Confirmation
- Eucharist
- Holy Orders
- Reconciliation
- Anointing of the Sick
- Matrimony

Which sacraments have you received?

things to think about

We read of God's plan for us in the Bible. The Church gives us the Sunday readings to guide our lives. Have you made the Sunday readings a part of your daily or weekly prayer? Look up the readings for this coming Sunday. Read them slowly, quietly, prayerfully. See if you can detect part of God's plan for you this week!

things to share

What is your part in God's plan? How do you think people your age can fulfill it right now? In what way does the Church help you to do this?

WORDS TO REMEMBER

Find and define the following:

sacrament _____
_____
_____

lectionary _____
_____
_____

OnLine WITH THE PARISH

Understanding the Scriptures has become increasingly important, both for our private prayer and for our celebration of the liturgy. Does your parish provide ways to study the Scripture? Are the Scripture readings for the week listed in the parish bulletin? Is there a parish library? Is there a Scripture discussion group for young people? If not, think about forming one.

What is a sacrament?

1

What do we mean when we say that Jesus fulfilled God's plan?

2

Name the seven sacraments.

3

Why is the reading of Scripture a necessary part of the liturgy?

4

Give a short definition for each of the following words:

berakah

anamnesis

epiclesis

5

Life
in the Spirit

The following prayer is in the form of a berakah:

Jesus, Good Shepherd,
you always show me the right path
when I take time to ask for your help.
Help me this week, especially when....

Find some quiet time this week, and make up your own berakah prayer. You may want to write your prayer on a good piece of paper, illustrate it or draw a frame around it, and post it in your room as your "prayer of the week."

CHAPTER 4

The Sacrament of Sacraments

The cup of blessing that we bless, is it not a participation in the blood of Christ?

The bread that we break, is it not a participation in the body of Christ?

I Corinthians 10:16

Why is it that we call one sacrament by so many names—Eucharist, the Lord's Supper, the breaking of Bread, the Holy Sacrifice, the sacred mysteries, Holy Communion, and Holy Mass? Why do you think this sacrament is so important?

Source and Summit

From the very first moments of the Church's life, it has been true. The Eucharist is the center of our lives. The early Christians knew this. That is why even under threat of persecution and death, they would risk their lives to come together and celebrate this sacrament. Hidden away in the catacombs or meeting secretly in people's homes, the early Christians knew why the celebration of the Eucharist was so important to them.

Contemporary Catholics know the same truth. All over the world, whenever and wherever the Mass is celebrated, Catholics will travel for miles just to receive Communion. We know that despite any suffering the Church may endure, men and women will still come together as a eucharistic assembly of faith.

Why is this so? What draws people to this sacrament? After all, it has not really changed that much in two thousand years. We still offer the simple gifts of bread and wine. We still gather around the priest who presides at each Mass. Let's take a moment to look more deeply at this sacrament of sacraments that the Church says is the source and summit of our life.

The Body and Blood of Christ

The first thing that Catholics must understand is that the sacrament of the *Eucharist* is really and truly the Body and Blood of Christ. The bread and wine are not just symbols to remind us of Christ. In the Eucharist they have become Christ—body and blood, soul and divinity. Jesus himself told us this. Even before the Last Supper, he said, "I am the living bread that came down from heaven; whoever eats this bread will live forever; and the bread that I will give is my flesh for the life of the world" (John 6:51).

He went on to say, "Unless you eat the flesh of the Son of Man and drink his blood, you do not have life within you. Whoever eats my flesh and drinks my blood has eternal life, and I will raise him on the last day. For my flesh is true food, and my blood is true drink" (John 6:53–55).

On the night before he died for us, Jesus instituted this sacrament of his Body and Blood. At the Passover feast commemorating God's saving action of bringing the Jewish people from death to life, Jesus took the gifts of unleavened bread and wine and said, "This is my body which will be given up for you. This is the cup of my blood, the blood of the new and everlasting covenant. Do this in memory of me." What had Jesus done? He had given to his Church a memorial of his saving passion, death, and resurrection. Now, for all time, his disciples could gather together in the presence of their risen Savior and once again enter into the paschal mystery. They could make themselves part of the one sacrifice of Jesus Christ and give praise to God the Father through him.

How wonderful! How simple and yet full of mystery. The Savior of the world would now be with his Church for all time in a most marvelous way. In this sacred meal the Church would be nourished as the body of Christ by Christ himself. In the liturgy the Church would give thanks—the meaning of Eucharist—for all that God had done through his Son. By the power of the Holy Spirit, the Church would unite itself to Christ by sharing in his Body and Blood.

So vital is this sacrament that we will spend two chapters exploring its meaning and celebration for our lives—even before looking at the other sacraments. We will be celebrating the Eucharist throughout our lives. How important it is, then, that we as mature Catholics realize how critical we are at the celebration of the Eucharist. When we assemble, we are Christ's body, the Church, and we make this reality visible. We are never more the Church than when we are celebrating the Eucharist around the table of the Lord. In this sacrament of love, our redemption is carried on, we are filled with grace, and a pledge of future glory is given to us (*Catechism,* 1402, 1405).

Our Time, God's Time

Remembering (anamnesis) is at the heart of each of the sacraments. This is especially true of the Eucharist. Every time we celebrate the Eucharist, we hear the words "Do this in memory of me." We remember what Jesus did on Holy Thursday at the Last Supper. We remember what he did for us on Calvary on the first Good Friday. We remember how he rose from the dead on Easter Sunday. Indeed we remember the entire life of Jesus, all that he said and did for us as our redeemer.

When we remember these events at the Eucharist, we do not merely think about events that happened long ago in Jerusalem. The liturgy makes them *present* to us here and now.

This kind of presence may be difficult to understand at first. We are used to thinking of time in a "straight line":

past time > present time > future time

It seems only common sense to chop time up this way. The past is what used to be; the future is what has not yet happened. Only *now* is truly real to us.

But imagine that you are looking at a house you have never seen before. If you are standing in front of the house, for example, you see only the front; you can only imagine what the back is like. If you are directly above the house, you have a completely different view, but you still do not see *all* of it. Time is something like that for us. We see only what is before us: the present. We can only read about the past; we can only imagine the future.

For God, however, our past, present, and future are all one. For God all time is *now.* This is a hint of what "God's time of salvation" means. In the liturgy the events we might think of as "past" are actually present. In the liturgy we do not just recall the events of Holy Thursday, Good Friday, and

Easter Sunday. These events are made present. This does not mean that these events are repeated. No. Only the celebrations are repeated. But "in each celebration there is an outpouring of the Holy Spirit that makes the unique mystery present" (*Catechism*, 1104). When we celebrate the liturgy, the mysteries of our faith are made present so that we may enter into the event. When we enter the story, we encounter the presence of Christ, and we are filled with God's grace. When we celebrate the liturgy, we stand in God's time and God's presence.

A Beautiful Balance

We must keep in balance the three mysteries—Holy Thursday, Good Friday, and Easter Sunday—and not let any one outweigh the others. A true Catholic understanding of the Eucharist is achieved only when we balance all three. If we think of the Mass as a meal but do not see the relation of the meal to Christ's sacrifice on Good Friday, we do not have a balanced understanding. If we reverence Christ present in the Eucharist but fail to reverence Christ present in the Church (in one another and in the poor), we do not have a balanced understanding of the Eucharist.

We begin with Good Friday in order to understand what we mean when we say the Mass is a *sacrifice.* Today when we think of sacrifice, we usually think of giving up something—giving up candy for Lent or giving up softball in order to play in the band. When we think of sacrifices in the Old Testament, we might picture the sacrifice of an animal.

In this kind of sacrifice, the blood of the animal was a symbol of life. On the Day of Atonement, the holiest of all Jewish feast days, the high priest sprinkled this blood on the assembled community. This ritual action was a sign that it was God's own life which gave life to the people. In the life the people now shared with God, their sins were forgiven; they were at one (*at-one-ment*) with God and with one another.

The emphasis in this ritual is, not on the killing of the animal, but on the celebration of *the people's joyful union with God.* The central meaning of sacrifice, then, is union with God, not death or giving something up. For the Hebrews, for Jesus, for the early Church, and for us today, *sacrifice* is a ritual action that brings about and celebrates our joyful union with God.

Crucifixion, Sadao Watanabe, 1970

Eucharist and Sacrifice

As the early followers of Jesus began to reflect on his death and resurrection, they began to understand the Good Friday event as a sacrifice. Jesus began to be seen as the Lamb of God and the paschal victim—slain, yes, but victorious in the end. Jesus broke the chains of death. Through his sacrifice our sins were forgiven and we were reunited with God. Only Jesus, the spotless victim, could have done this.

We believe that the celebration of the Eucharist makes present to us the sacrifice Jesus offered once and for all on the cross. At the Eucharist we remember Good Friday not merely as a story or an event from the past. The sacrifice of Jesus is a *mystery;* it is more than words can say. It is a mystery we remember and make present each time we celebrate the Eucharist.

CATHOLIC ID The words that Catholics use reflect what they believe about the Eucharist. Out of deep respect for Christ's real presence in the Eucharist, we call the consecrated Bread the *Host,* and the consecrated Wine the *Precious Blood.*

 Have you ever made a sacrifice that gave life, even in a small way?

47

"This is my body"

The Eucharistic Prayer

At each Eucharist we hear these or similar words:
   While they were at supper,
   he took bread, said the blessing, broke
      the bread,
   and gave it to his disciples, saying:
   Take this, all of you, and eat it:
   this is my body which will be given up for you.

What a wonderful phrase to reflect on: "my body which will be given up for you." In joining with Christ to celebrate this Holy Thursday meal, we celebrate and make present the sacrifice of Good Friday. Sacrifices are celebrated in many different ways. One form of sacrifice known to Jesus and the early Church was the sacred meal: Eating and drinking together symbolized and brought about joyful union with God.

Today, at the Holy Sacrifice of the Mass, the meal is the external sign of the sacrifice. We do not ask whether the Mass is a sacrifice *or* a meal; it is *both.* The sharing of food and drink, the meal itself, is the sacrament. It is the external sign of the sacrifice. What we *see* is a meal; what the meal *makes present* is the sacrifice.

Before meals most Catholics "say grace." They say a prayer thanking God for the food they are about to eat and asking God to bless them as they share their meal. At the Eucharist, the greatest of all meals, we say, through the priest, the eucharistic prayer, the greatest of all meal prayers.

The basic shape of this meal prayer is that of the prayer of blessing (berakah) known to Jesus and the apostles. This prayer, spoken in our name by the priest, involves three elements:

• We call upon the name of God (invocation).
• We gratefully remember all that God has done for us (anamnesis).
• We make our petition (epiclesis).

The eucharistic prayer begins with a dialogue between the priest and the people, "The Lord be with you. . . . Lift up your hearts. . . ." Then we call on God, our loving Father, and give thanks for all the wonderful things he has done for us. We thank God most especially for Jesus. We remember what Jesus did for us at the Last Supper; we remember his passion, death, and resurrection. And we make our petition. We ask God to send the Holy Spirit to change the bread and wine into the Body and Blood of Christ. We ask that we who eat the Bread and drink the Cup may become one body in that same Spirit.

When we listen closely to the words of the eucharistic prayer and understand the meaning of this greatest "grace before meals," we understand the relationship between Holy Thursday and the meaning of the Eucharist.

Meal and Sacrifice

To understand the Eucharist we must balance the Good Friday and Holy Thursday events. This is not always easy. *Sacrifice* suggests an altar; *meal* suggests a table. Can one object be both altar and table? Can we balance the reverence required by a sacrifice with the hospitality and warmth expected at a meal? Yes, we can. And we do, every time we celebrate the Eucharist.

At a sacrifice great care is taken that what is sacrificed is pure and spotless. At a meal we are concerned that the food is tasty and abundant. Can the bread we use for the Eucharist be both? At a meal we eat and drink; we take the food in our hands. How are these gestures balanced with the reverence required by a sacrifice?

Good Friday and Holy Thursday must be balanced in our reverence and devotion at the Eucharist. We are, as the hymn says, "kneeling at the foot of the cross." But we are also "sitting with Christ and the saints at the heavenly banquet, listening to Christ's words, sharing the bread and wine." The songs we sing at Mass speak not only of adoration but also of eating and drinking. We sing about meals, suppers, and banquets. Besides calling it "the Holy Sacrifice of the Mass," we also speak of "celebrating the Eucharist."

In order to understand the Eucharist well, we must hold the images of Good Friday and Holy Thursday in their proper balance. And to these two we add a third: the image of Easter Sunday.

Find a song about the Eucharist in a hymnal or a missalette. What does it say about a meal? a sacrifice?

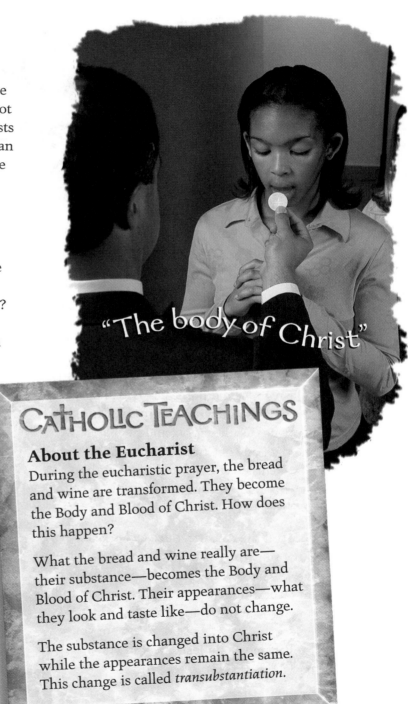

"The body of Christ"

CATHOLIC TEACHINGS

About the Eucharist

During the eucharistic prayer, the bread and wine are transformed. They become the Body and Blood of Christ. How does this happen?

What the bread and wine really are— their substance—becomes the Body and Blood of Christ. Their appearances—what they look and taste like—do not change.

The substance is changed into Christ while the appearances remain the same. This change is called *transubstantiation*.

Supper at Emmaus, Ivo Dulčič, 1916

I Am with You

At the end of Matthew's Gospel, Jesus tells us, "I am with you always, until the end of the age" (Matthew 28:20). The Eucharist is the celebration of this abiding presence of Jesus in our midst. When Jesus returned to heaven, he did not leave us orphans. The risen Jesus makes us one with him in the Church. Through Baptism, Confirmation, and Eucharist, we have become the body of Christ. This is the heart of Easter Sunday: Christ is totally identified with us, his followers, his Church. Our work now is to be the presence of Christ in the world.

This is what Paul the Apostle, once called Saul, learned on the road to Damascus. In the Acts of the Apostles we see Saul on his way to persecute the followers of Jesus. Suddenly, "he fell to the ground and heard a voice saying to him, 'Saul, Saul, why are you persecuting me?' He said, 'Who are you, sir?' The reply came, 'I am Jesus, whom you are persecuting'" (Acts 9:4–5).

This experience taught Paul that Christ cannot be separated from his members. The risen Lord is so united to us, his followers, that what we do to one another we do to Christ. This fact is central to our understanding of the real presence of Christ at the Eucharist. Paul met Christ who was so identified with us that to persecute Christians was to persecute Christ himself.

We Are One Body

Around A.D. 50, Paul wrote to the Corinthians regarding some concerns he had about the way they were celebrating the Eucharist. At issue was their understanding of the presence of Christ in the Eucharist.

He had no praise for the Corinthians in the way they celebrated the Eucharist. In fact he told them that their meetings were doing more harm than good. He had heard of the divisions between the rich and the poor that separated the community.

He told the Corinthians that when they gather for the Eucharist, "It is not to eat the Lord's supper, for in eating, each one goes ahead with his own supper, and one goes hungry while another gets drunk. Do you not have houses in which you can eat and drink? Or do you show contempt for the church of God and make those who have nothing feel ashamed?" (1 Corinthians 11:20–22).

Paul scolds the Corinthians for celebrating the Eucharist without recognizing the body of Christ—his Church. The poor are going hungry while the rich eat and drink all they want. His criticism of their eucharistic devotion goes to the heart of the matter, to the very meaning of the Eucharist. Nourished by Christ himself, we are to live as Jesus did and work for true justice and true peace. The Eucharist commits us to this.

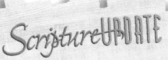

ScriptureUPDATE

In their gospels Matthew, Mark, and Luke describe the supper Jesus celebrated with his disciples on the night before he died. Each tells how Jesus took bread and wine, gave it to the disciples, and said, "This is my body; this is my blood."

These important words of Jesus do not appear in John's Gospel. Instead we read how Jesus "poured water into a basin and began to wash the disciples' feet" (John 13:5). What does Jesus say this action means? (See John 13:12–20.) What do you think Jesus' gesture tells us about the Eucharist?

Saint Paul tells the Corinthians that this is the "body of Christ" they must see at the Eucharist if they are to celebrate worthily. He reminded them that all who eat and drink without recognizing *this* body eat and drink judgment on themselves. Sharing the Eucharist is a promise that we will treat all people as Christ would treat them—indeed, as we would treat Christ himself. This is also what it means to "do this in memory of me."

So the next time you hear the words "Body of Christ" at Communion remember and believe that:

• Christ is our Lord and reigns forever in heaven.
• Christ is really and truly present in the Eucharist.
• We the Church are the body of Christ.

If we believe these things about the Eucharist, then the words of Saint Augustine can both make sense to us and challenge us: "We become what we eat"—that is, in the Eucharist we can be transformed into Christ.

How wonderful then is this sacrament of sacraments. Through it we are united with Christ. We are strengthened in holiness to keep free from sin. And we are united as the Church, the body of Christ.

  Why do you think it is so important to prepare to receive Christ in the Eucharist and to receive him worthily?

51

things
to think about

The next time you go to Mass, will the images of Holy Thursday, Good Friday, and Easter Sunday play a part in your thoughts and prayers? Will you picture yourself at table with Jesus? How can you be more aware of those around you and of the ways that together you form the body of Christ? How will the poor and those in need fit into your celebration? Write your thoughts in your journal.

things
to share

Ask a longtime Catholic to talk with you about the Eucharist. Ask, "How do you pray during Sunday Mass?" "What does the Eucharist mean to you?" Think about his or her responses. Are the ideas of meal (Holy Thursday), sacrifice (Good Friday), and real presence (Easter Sunday) expressed?

Talk to some of your churchgoing Christian friends. Ask them to describe what their Sunday worship services are like. How does their worship compare with what we Catholics do on Sunday?

WORDS TO REMEMBER

Find and define the following:

sacrifice _____
_____
_____

Eucharist _____
_____
_____

OnLine
WITH THE PARISH

The arrangement of each parish church reflects an understanding of the Eucharist celebrated there. Look around your parish church to see which furnishings and decorations emphasize Holy Thursday, Good Friday, and Easter Sunday. Is there a large crucifix over the altar, or is there an image of the risen Christ? Do you think the altar/table looks more like an altar for sacrifice or like a table for a meal? Does it look like both?

Why is the Mass a sacrifice? At the Eucharist how do we remember and make present the event of Good Friday?

1

Why is the Mass a meal? At the Eucharist how do we remember and make present the event of Holy Thursday?

2

How is Christ present at the Eucharist? At the Eucharist how do we remember and make present the event of Easter Sunday?

3

What do we promise when we receive the Body of Christ at the Eucharist?

4

What is our petition during the eucharistic prayer?

5

Life in the Spirit

The songs, chants, and hymns we sing at the Eucharist help us to celebrate with meaning. Think about some of your favorite hymns or liturgical songs. Copy a verse or two from one of them into your journal. What does this verse say to you about the meaning of the Eucharist? Why do you think it appeals to you? Do you know it by heart? This week, try using your verse as a starting point for prayer or meditation, or call it to mind frequently as you go about your day.

CHAPTER 5

Celebrating Eucharist

He was made known to them in the breaking of the bread.

Luke 24:35

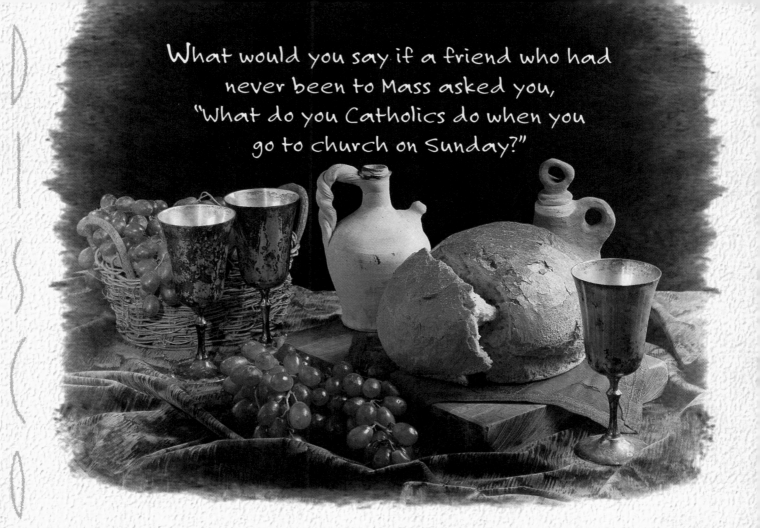

What would you say if a friend who had never been to Mass asked you, "What do you Catholics do when you go to church on Sunday?"

Owning the Eucharist

Most of us have been celebrating the Eucharist almost all our lives, so we may think we know it well. This chapter, however, may open our eyes to the Eucharist in a new way. By learning more about the elements of the Eucharist, we can more clearly understand how best we can think, pray, and act during the celebration. We can better own the Eucharist, enter into it, as *our* celebration.

Of course none of this would matter so much if the Eucharist were an action we simply watched as spectators. But the Eucharist is a community action, a liturgical action. It requires the participation of each and every one of us, the entire body of Christ.

"Doing" is different from just "watching." Doing requires information and skills. Playing the trumpet in the band requires more information and skills than standing on the curb, watching the parade go

by. At the Eucharist we are the "players"; we *all* celebrate the Eucharist together. We each have an active part, whether that be reading, listening, bringing up the gifts, singing, or responding together with our "Amen!" In the last chapter we studied what the Eucharist means. Now we want to learn how to celebrate that meaning.

The external shape of the Mass is a meal. It will help us understand how to celebrate the Eucharist if we first think of what we do when we celebrate a special meal in our homes. For example, how might you celebrate Thanksgiving dinner at your grandmother's house?

Each person's Thanksgiving might be a little different, but we would probably find these same four parts in any meal of celebration: (1) We gather. (2) We tell our stories. (3) We share our meal by putting food on the table, saying the blessing, and eating and drinking. (4) We return home.

The Eucharistic Meal The Eucharistic meal has a similar four-fold structure:

- gathering
- storytelling
- meal sharing: preparation of the gifts, the eucharistic prayer, the communion rite
- commissioning

Each of these elements has its own special purpose. The better we understand each of these four parts of the Eucharist, the better will we be able to celebrate the Eucharist with meaning.

Gathering

We come together in one place for the eucharistic assembly. We gather together as the Church to make the body of Christ visible.

The priest invites us to make the sign of the cross. He greets us, saying "The Lord be with you." We respond, "And also with you." This greeting is used several times during the Mass. It is intended both as a wish, meaning "*May* the Lord be with you" and as a profound statement of faith, meaning "As you assemble for worship, the Lord *is* with you." This is an ancient greeting, found frequently in the Old Testament. It is a blessing that we exchange among ourselves in our everyday lives, although we may not realize it. This blessing, our familiar "good-bye," is a shortened form of "God be with you."

This greeting and all the other ritual acts of these Introductory Rites are intended *to gather us together into a worshiping assembly.* We are asked to pause and recall our common need for salvation (the penitential rite). On Sundays and feasts, we sing or recite the hymn "Glory to God in the highest." The "Gloria" has been part of the Mass since the sixth century.

At the close of these rites that gather us together, the priest asks us to join our hearts and minds in prayer. After a few moments of silence the priest "collects" our intentions into one prayer. We make it our own by responding "Amen."

When we gather to celebrate the Eucharist, we gather to experience the presence of Christ. This reality begins even during this first part of the Eucharist, the Introductory Rites. Here we experience together what Christ has promised: "Where two or three are gathered together in my name, there am I in the midst of them" (Matthew 18:20).

Storytelling

When we gather for a meal, we usually begin with conversation: telling our stories. At the Eucharist, after the Introductory Rites, we sit down and enter into the ritual of conversation with Sacred Scripture, the inspired word of God. We do this in the Liturgy of the Word.

Through the reading of the Scriptures, we listen to the Father's story once again. As we hear God's story, we are reminded of our own stories, our own hopes and dreams. As we grow and change from day to day, we listen to the Scriptures from a slightly different perspective. At every liturgy, we are given the opportunity to hear God's story in a new way.

On Sundays we have three such opportunities, because there are three readings. The first reading is ordinarily taken from the Old Testament, and is related in theme to the gospel of the day. This Old Testament reading recalls, in some way, God the Father's original covenant with us. Following the first reading we sing or recite a psalm, a song from God's own inspired hymnal, the Book of Psalms. The second reading is usually from one of the letters of Paul or from another apostolic writing. The first two readings conclude with "The word of the Lord." To this we all respond with our liturgical "yes" as we say, "Thanks be to God."

The third reading is taken from one of the four gospels. Because of the unique respect given to the gospel words of Jesus, it has long been the custom in the Church to stand in attentive reverence during the proclamation of the gospel.

Before proclaiming the gospel, the priest greets us with "The Lord be with you." As he announces the particular gospel of the day, he traces with his right thumb a series of three small crosses on his forehead, on his lips, and on his heart. Silently he prays that God will cleanse his mind and his heart so that his lips may proclaim the gospel worthily. In many places the congregation makes these small signs of the cross along with the priest. The gospel reading concludes with, "The gospel of the Lord." We respond, "Praise to you, Lord Jesus Christ." We thus proclaim our faith in the presence of Christ in the word. Then we sit for the homily.

The *homily* takes the word of God and brings it to our life today. Just as a large piece of bread must be broken to be eaten, a good homily "breaks open" the word of God in order that we might hear, understand, and act upon it.

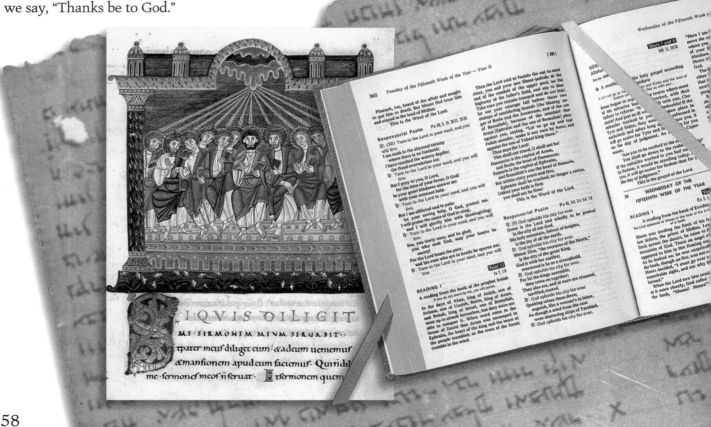

General Intercessions The Liturgy of the Word comes to a close with what are called the general intercessions.

At Mass, the general intercessions help us recall that we are the body of Christ by Baptism. Now, as we prepare to approach the table for Eucharist, we look into the readings as we would look into a mirror. We examine the picture of Christ and the Church presented in the Scripture. Does our assembly, the body of Christ present here, resemble that picture? In the general intercessions, we pray that we will really come to look like the body of Christ proclaimed in the Scripture: a body at peace, providing shelter for the homeless, healing for the sick, and food for the hungry.

In the general intercessions, we pray that our Church and our world might come to look like the plan God has for us. Our petitions usually fall into four categories: the needs of the universal Church, all nations and their leaders, people in special need, and the needs of our local parish. As these petitions are announced, we all pray for these intentions in our hearts. Then we make our common response aloud: "Lord, hear our prayer."

What will you pray for so that your parish community will "reflect" the body of Christ proclaimed in the Scripture?

A good homily helps us connect God's story with our own lives. The homily is often followed by a few moments of silence. We take this time to thank God for the word we have heard and to consider how we can apply the readings and the homily to our lives.

On Sundays we then stand and together recite the Nicene Creed. The creed is a statement of our faith in the word we have heard proclaimed in the Scripture and the homily.

Originally the creed was the profession of faith of those to be baptized at this point in the Mass. Today the creed reminds us of our own Baptism. As we make our profession of faith, we are reminded that each time we come to the Eucharist, we come through Baptism.

Scripture UPDATE

In Luke's Gospel we read the story of two disciples on the road to Emmaus. This story is the source of the fourfold structure we are using to understand the Mass. Read Luke 24:13–35 in your Bible. See if you can identify the four movements:

• Who gathers?

• What stories do they tell?

• Where do they recognize the presence of the risen Lord?

• What do they do at the end of the story, "after Mass"?

Preparation of the Gifts

The Dialogue

Meal Sharing

Following the Liturgy of the Word, we move to the table of the Lord. In any meal celebration there are three movements: We bring the food to the table, say grace, and share the food. At Mass these actions are called the preparation of the gifts, the eucharistic prayer, and the communion rite.

Preparation of the Gifts   Members of the community bring the bread and wine for the Eucharist to the priest at the altar. Then begins the preparation of the gifts. The priest places the bread and wine on the table. He mixes water with wine and washes his hands. These gestures remind us of the Last Supper: Mixing water with the wine and washing hands were rituals the Jews followed at all meals in Jesus' time. The priest then invites us to pray that our sacrifice be acceptable to God. We respond "Amen" to the prayer over the gifts and stand to participate in the central prayer of the Mass.

The Eucharistic Prayer

The eucharistic prayer brings us to the very center of the Mass and to the heart of our Catholic faith. The structure of this prayer is that of a berakah:

1. We call upon God the Father to remember all the wonderful saving deeds of our history.

2. We then recall Jesus Christ and, in particular, the memorial he left us on the night before he died. We narrate the institution of the Eucharist at the Last Supper, and we recall (anamnesis) his passion, death, and resurrection.

3. Then as we gratefully (eucharist) remember all the wonderful saving acts God has done for us in the past, we petition (epiclesis) the Father to send the Spirit to continue those deeds of Christ in the present and future. Now let us see how the berakah is expressed at Mass.

The Dialogue   The eucharistic prayer begins with a dialogue between the priest and the assembly: "The Lord be with you…." The priest then asks if we are ready and willing to approach the table, to renew our baptismal commitment, to offer ourselves to God: "Lift up your hearts." And we say that we are prepared to do so: "We lift them up to the Lord." The priest invites us to give thanks to the Lord our God. And we respond: "It is right to give him thanks and praise." (The word *eucharist* comes from the Greek, "to give thanks and praise.")

The Preface   The priest begins the preface. In most cases *preface* means simply an introduction. Here *preface* retains its original meaning of speaking in the presence of God. We are brought into God's presence and speak directly to God, thanking him for his wonderful works. We ask to join the choirs of angels, who praise God unendingly in the heavenly liturgy. We cannot hold back our joy, and sing aloud with them:

> Holy, holy, holy Lord, God of power and might, heaven and earth are full of your glory.

Epiclesis   The priest continues the eucharistic prayer, giving praise and thanks. He then invokes the Father (epiclesis) to send the Holy Spirit to change our gifts of bread and wine into the Body and Blood of Christ.

Epiclesis

Consecration and Anamnesis

Doxology

We also pray that we who take part in this Eucharist may become one body and one spirit. Only then can we experience the fullest presence of Christ.

Anamnesis The priest recalls the events of the Last Supper and the story of the institution of the Eucharist. (These words are called the "words of consecration.") He then speaks to us, inviting us to "proclaim the mystery of faith." Among the choices given for this acclamation, a short and familiar one is:

> Christ has died,
> Christ is risen,
> Christ will come again.

The priest continues to recall with us (anamnesis) the wonderful deeds which saved us: the passion, death, and resurrection of Christ.

Epiclesis for Unity The grateful memory of God's salvation leads us to make the second half of our petition—our primary petition (epiclesis) at every Eucharist—the petition for unity. In the second eucharistic prayer we pray:

> May all of us who share in the body and blood of Christ
> be brought together in unity by the Holy Spirit.

We look forward to that glorious feast of never-ending joy in heaven and join our voices with those of all the saints who have gone before us as the priest raises the bread and wine and offers a doxology, a prayer of glory to God in the name of Christ:

> Through him,
> with him,
> in him,
> in the unity of the Holy Spirit,
> all glory and honor is yours,
> almighty Father,
> for ever and ever.

Our "Amen" to this prayer acclaims our assent and participation in the entire eucharistic prayer.

Look back at the parts of the eucharistic prayers on these pages. What do you think we are saying "yes" to in each of the parts?

CATHOLIC TEACHINGS

About the Mass

It is Christ himself, acting through the ministry of priests, who offers the eucharistic sacrifice. Only validly ordained priests can preside at the Eucharist and consecrate the bread and wine. Through Baptism, however, all of us share in the priesthood of Christ. This is called "the common priesthood of the faithful." Laypeople may take on special roles in the liturgy, serving as readers, altar servers, and eucharistic ministers.

61

The Communion Rite

The meal sharing or Liturgy of the Eucharist consists of three parts: the preparation of the gifts, the eucharistic prayer, both of which we have already studied, and the communion rite, to which we now turn.

We prepare to eat and drink at the Lord's table by praying together the Lord's Prayer: "Give us this day our daily bread; and forgive us our trespasses as we forgive those who trespass against us."

Communion is the sign and source of our reconciliation and union with God and with one another. Therefore, we make a gesture of union and forgiveness with those around us and offer them a sign of peace.

The priest then shows us the Bread and Cup and invites us to come to the table:

> This is the Lamb of God ....
> Happy are those who are called to his supper.

Here we are once more reminded that the Mass is both a sacrifice and a meal. We come forward to eat and drink the Body and Blood of Christ.

As God fed our Hebrew ancestors in the desert on their pilgrimage to the promised land, so God gives us food for our journey today. We approach the minister, who gives us the eucharistic Bread with the words "The body of Christ." We respond "Amen." We then go to the minister with the Cup who offers it to us with the words "The blood of Christ," to which we again profess our "Amen."

During this procession we usually sing a hymn which unites our voices, thoughts, and spirits, even as the Body and Blood of Christ unites us as one body in Christ. Then we pray silently in our hearts, asking for all that this sacrament promises. The priest unites our prayers in the prayer after Communion, to which we respond "Amen."

Commissioning

Finally we prepare to go back to that world in which we work and play, study and live. The burdens we have laid down at the door of the church for this Eucharist we know we must take up again. But now we bear them with the strength received from this Eucharist and this community. The priest again says "The Lord be with you," this ritual phrase serving now as a farewell.

As the bread and wine are brought to the altar, we picture ourselves sitting at table with Jesus at the Last Supper. We become present to that moment and give thanks. As we listen to the eucharistic prayer and ask the Holy Spirit to make us one, we remember Jesus' own prayer: "I pray.... Father.... that they may be one, as we are one" (John 17:20–22).

We place ourselves at the foot of the cross and offer our lives to God. We promise God that we will do his will, even as Jesus did on Calvary.

We say the Lord's Prayer and ask forgiveness for our sins. We step forward to share in the eucharistic meal, which is past (the Last Supper), present (Christ's living presence today), and future (a foretaste of the banquet of heaven).

We bow our heads to receive a blessing. As the priest blesses us in the name of the Trinity, we make the sign of the cross as we did at the beginning of the Mass. The priest or deacon then dismisses the assembly: "Go in peace to love and serve the Lord." And we give our liturgical "yes" as we say "Thanks be to God."

Strengthened by this meal, we are commissioned to go forth and be bread for the world.

 *Reflect for a moment. Decide on one way you will go forth from the Eucharist to be "bread" for someone.*

A Personal Overview

How do we celebrate the Eucharist? We see that the answer to this question depends on what part of the Eucharist we are celebrating. During the time of gathering we become aware that together with all those around us we are the body of Christ. During the storytelling we listen attentively to the words of Sacred Scripture and enter into the story. During the homily we learn how the Scriptures apply to our lives today. During the general intercessions we pray that God's story might become real for us.

 CATHOLIC ID

Do you know that we Catholics consider the Eucharist a sacrament of reconciliation? The Church tells us that when we receive the Eucharist worthily our venial sins are forgiven. The Eucharist strengthens our love for God, self, and others, and this love wipes out sin. The Eucharist also preserves us from future sin. "The more we share the life of Christ and progress in his friendship, the more difficult it is to break away from him...." (*Catechism*, 1395). Forgiveness of sin springs from the principal effect of the Eucharist in our lives: union with Christ.

PUTTING IT ON TOGETHER

things to think about

Does "going to Mass" mean that we simply watch what the priest does? Celebrating the Eucharist requires that we know how to join together with others. We must know how to listen. We must know how to give and receive signs of forgiveness, and how to say thank you.

How do you join with others at Mass? How could you become a better listener?

things to share

With several of your friends, recall a time when you really enjoyed celebrating a liturgy—when it was especially meaningful for you. As you tell your story and listen to the stories of your friends, ask what it was about these liturgies that made them "good." How do the things that make liturgy a good experience relate to the things which we have studied in this chapter?

WORDS TO REMEMBER

Find and define the following:

preface _____

_____

_____

communion _____

_____

_____

OnLine WITH THE PARISH

Does your parish need readers, singers, ushers, or altar servers? Sacristans (those who help prepare the altar for Mass) may be needed, too. Volunteer your help. Often parishes offer training sessions for these ministries. Does yours? When we each do our part well, we help the whole parish to celebrate the Eucharist together in the best possible way.

How would you respond if a friend who had never been to Mass asked you, "What do you Catholics do when you go to church on Sunday?"

1

What do we remember in the eucharistic prayer? What do we ask for?

2

Name the elements of the Introductory Rites. What is their purpose?

3

What is the purpose of the general intercessions?

4

How is the eucharistic meal a celebration which is past, present, and future?

5

Life in the Spirit

Why do we pray the Our Father at the Eucharist? Because Jesus himself gave us these words to pray. As adopted children of God, we, like Jesus, can also call God "our Father." The Our Father is the best "prayer before Communion" that the Church could possibly pray, for when we pray the Our Father, we are in *communion* with the Father, with his Son, Jesus Christ, and with the entire body of Christ, the Church.

Pray the Our Father quietly. Choose one phrase, like "Our Father," "thy will be done," or "forgive us our trespasses." Try to recall it during the week and the next time you receive the Eucharist.

CHAPTER 6

The Sacraments
of Initiation

I am the light of the world.
Whoever follows me will not walk in
darkness, but will have the light of life.

John 8:12

Think about one new beginning you might already have made in your life. Was it hard? Did you have help? Has it made your life better? What beginnings are you looking forward to?

Beginnings

How do you begin to become a Catholic? This probably doesn't seem to be a very important question if you already are a Catholic! Many of us were baptized when we were infants and have been Catholics ever since. In fact, since the earliest times, Baptism has been administered to infants and children. This continues today. But even so, the question of becoming Catholic is very important. That is because the *process* by which an unbaptized person becomes a Catholic is like a map that helps us understand how to follow Jesus.

The Church realizes that people coming to the Catholic faith as adults need a different kind of preparation, the kind that the early Church gave to the first converts from paganism. This preparation is called the *Rite of Christian Initiation of Adults (RCIA)*. Through the liturgies and prayers it provides, the RCIA prepares adults and young people to become members of the Catholic Church. Sometimes this preparation can last one or two

years. These new Catholics are initiated into the Church by receiving the three *sacraments of initiation*—Baptism, Confirmation, and Eucharist—all at once, usually at the Easter Vigil. So understanding the RCIA is a good way to understand the three sacraments of initiation.

We have already studied the meaning of the Eucharist. Yet we will continue our study in this chapter because Eucharist is so closely connected to Baptism and Confirmation. Every time we come to the Eucharist, we come "through Baptism." (This is why we dip our fingers into the baptismal water and make the sign of the cross when we enter a church.) At each Eucharist we renew the promises of our Baptism: the promises to renounce evil and to follow Christ.

In order to understand our baptismal promises, we first need to learn about conversion. *Conversion* is a key word that is important for an understanding of the sacraments. *Conversion* is the process of

coming to believe that Jesus Christ is the Savior of the world. The word literally means "turning around, going in the other direction." This helps us understand the meaning of the following related words: "convert," "repent," "do penance."

Conversion may seem to be something that we do. But even more important, it is something that *God* does. Faith in Christ—coming to believe that Jesus is the Savior of the world—is a gift. It is God's free gift. It is Jesus who calls us to conversion: "This is the time of fulfillment. The kingdom of God is at hand. Repent, and believe in the gospel" (Mark 1:15).

If conversion is a turning around, what do we *turn from*? What do we *turn toward*? Saint Paul tells us we are to *turn from* the flesh, all that is selfish, all that seeks "me first" without considering what God wants, all that is sinful. We are to *turn toward* the spirit, all that is life-giving and selfless, all that is generous, all that is filled with the Holy Spirit.

Conversion is a lifelong task. Baptism is our first "turning," or act of conversion, but this process continues throughout our lives. Conversion "is an uninterrupted task for the whole Church" (*Catechism*, 1428). This task is made possible by the paschal mystery of Jesus Christ.

We have learned that the celebration of the paschal mystery lies at the heart of every sacrament. This is especially true of Christian initiation. The sacraments of Baptism, Confirmation, and Eucharist can be thought of as one "moment." When we celebrate this moment, we signify our turning from selfishness and sin to a life in the Spirit of Christ Jesus. We can then say with Saint Paul: "I live, no longer I, but Christ lives in me" (Galatians 2:20).

As we look at the steps a person would take to become a Catholic, the process described in the RCIA, ask yourself these questions: "Am I turning more and more toward Jesus and the Spirit?" "Where am I on my road?" "Am I following this road map?"

Becoming a Catholic

When an unbaptized person wants to become a Catholic or to see what the Catholic Church is all about, he or she usually seeks out a parish and participates in a series of inquiry evenings or information sessions. In some cases, moved by the grace of the Holy Spirit, the person might decide to take the first formal steps toward becoming a Catholic. This is called becoming a catechumen, or entering the catechumenate. The catechumenate has four parts: instruction, moral conversion, worship, and ministry.

The root meaning of *catechumenate* is instruction. *Instruction* is the first step, an important part of the catechumenate. A person who wants to become a Catholic will naturally want to know what Catholics know. Above all, a catechumen must know Jesus and his Church.

The second step along the journey is "changing one's way of life," or *moral conversion*. This part of the process concerns morality, right and wrong behavior. As we come to know Jesus, we will want to act like Jesus. We will want to convert, "to turn around" and follow Jesus.

Worship is the third step along the way. Part of becoming a Catholic is worshiping together with Catholics, praying in a Catholic way. Catechumens will usually participate in Sunday Mass. They will leave after the homily in order to continue their reflection on the word of God while the baptized community celebrates the Eucharist. Until they are baptized, catechumens are not able to participate fully in the Eucharist.

This worship step of the catechumenate normally leads to the fourth step: *ministry*. Those who know Jesus will want to tell others about Jesus. They will want to share their faith and serve others in his name.

 Have you ever felt called to conversion, to changing your way of life? What did you do about it?

Initiation

There comes a day when a catechumen decides to ask for the sacraments of initiation: Baptism, Confirmation, and Eucharist. Because the catechumen chooses or elects the Church and the Church chooses or elects the individual, the catechumens are now called the elect. The *Rite of Election* takes place on the first Sunday of Lent.

The season of Lent is a season of spiritual retreat during which the catechumens prepare for their reception of Baptism, Confirmation, and First Eucharist at the Easter Vigil. It is a time for those who are already baptized to encourage the catechumens, and to pray with them. At the Easter Vigil, the Saturday night before Easter, all that the catechumens have been preparing for comes together.

A *vigil* is a time to wait and watch. The liturgy begins after nightfall. We gather around the Easter fire and listen to Scriptures that call to mind the wonder of our salvation. We shout forth our alleluia, which is fresh and new because we have not used it during the forty days of Lent. And we hear in the gospel the proclamation that Jesus has risen from the dead.

Rite of Acceptance into the Order of Cathechumens: presenting the gospels

Now the waiting and watching are over. The elect come forward, and we pray that what happened to Christ may now happen to them. They go down into the baptismal water, down into the tomb with Jesus: They are baptized. They emerge from the baptismal pool dripping wet with new life. The newly baptized are then clothed with a white garment, symbolizing that they have "clothed [themselves] with Christ" (Galatians 3:27). They are given candles lit from the Easter candle. Then they are anointed with oil: They are confirmed.

The vigil comes to its climax with the celebration of the Eucharist. The newly initiated join us for the first time at the table of the Lord.

CATHOLIC ID

The ordinary minister of Baptism is a bishop, priest, or deacon. But did you know that in case of necessity, anyone can baptize? In an emergency a person baptizes by pouring water over the head of the one to be baptized while saying, "I baptize you in the name of the Father, and of the Son, and of the Holy Spirit."

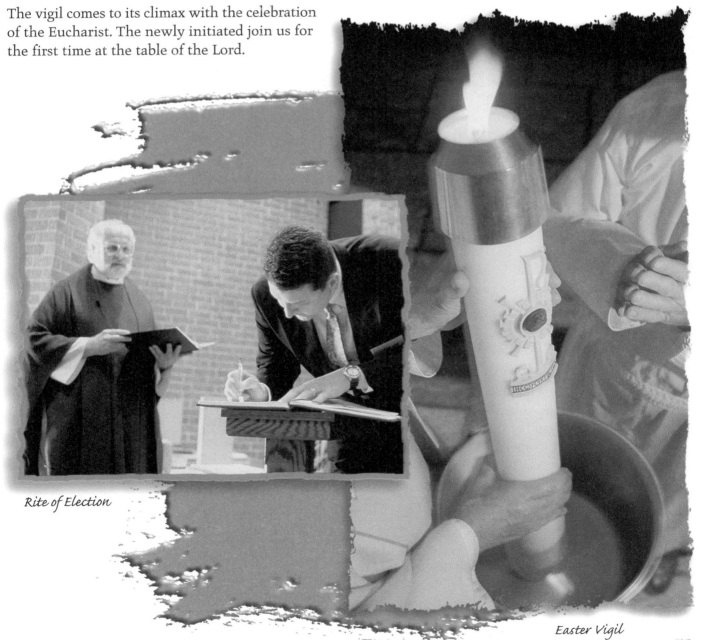

Rite of Election

Easter Vigil

Baptism

Baptism is so important. It is the gateway to the Christian life. In the New Testament Christian initiation is described by means of many symbols and images. Baptism is "being born again." As Jesus said to Nicodemus, "No one can see the kingdom of God without being born from above" (John 3:3). The experience of those emerging from the waters of Baptism is an experience of birth. At our human birth we came forth from the waters of our mother's womb and were born into a human family. We were welcomed and loved and received our family name.

In this sacrament we come forth from the waters of Baptism and are born into God's family. We are filled with the Spirit of love, welcomed by the Christian community, and receive the family name "Christian." We start afresh. All our sins—original sin and all personal sins—are taken away.

Baptism is also a "dying." In Baptism we go down into the tomb. The baptismal font itself can be seen as a symbol of both the womb, which brings forth life, and the tomb, a place of death. In baptism we are buried with Christ. We die to selfishness and sin so that the Spirit of Christ might be born in us.

Baptism is "seeing things in a new light." We emerge from the waters of Baptism and see things with God's eyes. We see a world in which we are no longer alone, a world in which we are connected with every other creature. We see a world in which we are no longer left to ourselves, a world in which we are loved and given power by the Spirit of God.

Baptism is "being adopted into a new family," the family of God. As family members we are brothers and sisters of Jesus Christ. We inherit everything that God has given to his own Son, especially the great gift of eternal life.

Through these baptismal images the Church has come to believe that "Baptism is the basis of the whole Christian life, the gateway to life in the Spirit . . . and the door which gives access to the other sacraments" (*Catechism*, 1213). Through Baptism we are made members of Christ and members of his body, the Church. We are in Christ and Christ is in us. His work, his mission in the world, is now our own.

 Which image of Baptism has greatest meaning for you? Why?

Celebrating Baptism

Another way we can learn the meaning of Baptism is by participating in the celebration of the sacraments of initiation, paying careful attention to both prayers and actions.

We have learned that the principal prayer of each sacrament is often expressed as a prayer of blessing (berakah): (1) We call God by name, "Father." (2) We gratefully remember what God has done for us. (3) We invoke the Holy Spirit.

At Baptism the blessing of the water takes this form. The priest moves to the water and calls upon God. He prays that the Father will give us grace through the sign of the gift of water. As the prayer continues, we remember (anamnesis) God's saving acts, especially those involving water. Then we make our petition:

> We ask you, Father, with your Son
> to send the Holy Spirit upon the waters
>   of this font.
> May all who are buried with Christ in the
>   death of baptism
> rise also with him to newness of life.

The candidates are plunged into this water three times (or water is poured over their heads three times), and the priest baptizes them in the name of the Father, and of the Son, and of the Holy Spirit.

This triple immersion gives the sacrament its name, for to baptize comes from a Greek word that means "to plunge" or "to immerse." Here the water is a symbol of Christ's death, and rising up from it is a symbol that the newly baptized person is risen with Christ and is now all new.

CATHOLIC TEACHINGS

About Baptism

Sometimes people may worry about those who die without being baptized. The Church teaches that those who have not been baptized but who die for the faith receive the grace of Baptism by their martyrdom. This is called the *Baptism of blood*. Unbaptized people who die, if they are catechumens or people who have sincerely tried to do the will of God, even without knowing the Church, are saved by what is called the *Baptism of desire*.

Baptism and clothing with white garment

Confirmation

At the Easter Vigil the sacraments of initiation are celebrated together in one liturgy. The meaning of each of the three sacraments is found in the meaning of the other two and in the meaning of the whole ceremony. Catholics who were baptized as infants receive Confirmation later, usually at a time when they can understand what the sacrament means.

Before we study the meaning of Confirmation as a separate sacrament, we must know something of its history. The ceremonies for Baptism and Confirmation were influenced by Roman bathing practices. In second-century Rome, the body would be rubbed with oil after a bath to moisturize the skin. In a similar way the bath of Baptism is followed by an anointing with oil, the sacrament of Confirmation.

We do not find many writings about Confirmation dating from the early days of the Church because it was thought of as part of Baptism. When they spoke of Baptism, the early Christians meant Baptism-Confirmation. Baptism is the washing; Confirmation is the anointing.

Baptism washes away sin and frees us from original sin. *Original sin* was the rejection of God by our first parents, resulting in the loss of sanctifying grace. With their sin, Adam and Eve deprived themselves and all their descendants of the original state of grace given by God. Because of original sin, we need to be saved by Jesus and restored to God's grace.

Original sin and sanctifying grace exist in a relationship similar to that of a vacuum and air. A vacuum is not something; rather, it is the absence of something—air.

Original sin is like that. It is the absence of something—God's grace.

Like a vacuum, original sin can best be understood by looking, not at what it is, but at what it is the absence of, what it is in need of.

The great vacuum of original sin is removed when the person begins to share in God's own life through the power of the Holy Spirit. This is what we call *sanctifying grace*. In God, the source of all holiness, we share in holiness.

Baptism and Confirmation exist in a similar relation: Baptism washes away original sin and fills us with grace; Confirmation seals us with the Spirit, strengthening the grace of Baptism.

What is original sin the absence of? What is taken away by Baptism? What is given by Confirmation?

The Effects of Initiation

It is important to remember that Confirmation and Baptism go together. Confirmation is saying yes to our Baptism, and this is the same yes we say each day of our ongoing conversion and especially each time that we celebrate the Eucharist. Baptism changes us so radically that we can never be "unbaptized." Baptism makes us members of Christ's body, and this change is so radical that it can never be undone. It is an indelible spiritual mark, or character, that cannot be taken away.

Confirmation strengthens and continues our Baptism. We receive the Holy Spirit in a special way. We are incorporated more firmly into Christ. Like Baptism, Confirmation marks us with an indelible character. The sacrament never needs to be repeated—nor can it be.

A good way to understand Confirmation is to look at the way the Church celebrates it. First, the bishop extends his hands over you (the typical gesture of invoking the Holy Spirit). Then, as he lays his hand on your head, he anoints your forehead with oil (remember that the name *Christ* means the "anointed one") and says, "Be sealed with the Gift of the Holy Spirit."

In Confirmation we are anointed with oil. It is a sign of consecration. We are anointed in order to share more fully in the mission of Jesus Christ. We are anointed as a sign that we have the seal of the Holy Spirit. Now we belong totally to Christ; we are enrolled in his service forever.

Scripture UPDATE

Very often during the rite of Confirmation, you may hear these words of Jesus about the Holy Spirit: "The Advocate, the holy Spirit that the Father will send in my name—he will teach you everything" (John 14:26). Here are a few more Scriptures from the rite of Confirmation. What do they say about the Holy Spirit in your life?

Luke 4:16–22   John 7:37–39

things to think about

We have seen that conversion is an ongoing process. Each day we continue to turn from all that is selfish and to turn toward all that is Spirit-filled and life-giving.

Can you name objects or activities in the life of a person your age that would be selfish in this context? Can you name objects or activities that are Spirit-filled?

things to share

Try the following experiment with your group: Close your eyes and say to yourself "Baptism." Then, with an imaginary camera, take a picture of the image that forms in your mind. Develop this imaginary picture and then describe it to your friends: For example, who is being baptized in this picture? How many people are present? How much water is there? How much oil? How much bread and wine?

WORDS TO REMEMBER

Find and define the following:

sacraments of initiation _____
_____
_____

conversion _____
_____
_____

OnLine

WITH THE PARISH

When are baptisms scheduled in your parish? Are infants baptized during Sunday Mass? When is Confirmation celebrated in your diocese? How old do you have to be to be confirmed in your diocese?

Sometimes the names of new Catholics are printed in the parish bulletin. Can you think of a way to make them feel welcome? You may wish to invite them to a prayer service on the theme of the sacraments of initiation.

1. What would you say if one of your friends who has never been baptized asked you, "How could I become a Catholic?" Include *catechumenate, RCIA,* and *sacraments of initiation* in your answer.

2. What are the four important steps along the road to conversion? Give a short definition for each.

3. What are the principal effects of Baptism?

4. What are the principal effects of Confirmation?

5. Choose one of the images of Baptism given in this chapter and explain what it tells us about the meaning of Christian initiation.

Life in the Spirit

Celebrate and renew your Baptism (and prepare for Confirmation if you have not already received it) by collecting prayers to the Holy Spirit in your journal. The prayer Come, Holy Spirit may already be familiar to you. Here is an ancient prayer to the Holy Spirit from the tradition of the Eastern Church. You might like to include it in your collection:

Heavenly King, Comforter, Spirit of Truth, you are everywhere present and filling all things. Treasury of Blessings and Giver of Life, come and dwell within us, cleanse us of all sin, and save our souls, O Good One.

CHAPTER 7

Our House of Prayer

LORD, I love the house where you dwell,
the tenting-place of your glory.

Psalm 26:8

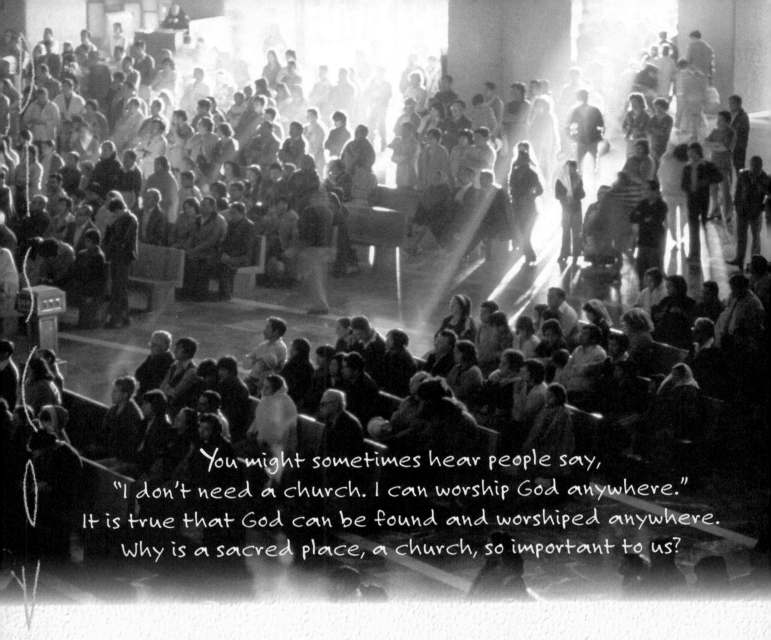

You might sometimes hear people say,
"I don't need a church. I can worship God anywhere."
It is true that God can be found and worshiped anywhere.
Why is a sacred place, a church, so important to us?

A Temple of Living Stones

Jesus himself needed and respected sacred space. He often found his own sacred space in "a deserted place" (Mark 1:35) where he prayed quietly alone. But he also gathered in places of worship with others. At the age of twelve, he went on pilgrimage with his parents to the Temple in Jerusalem (Luke 2:41). As an adult he prayed in the synagogue on the Sabbath "according to his custom" (Luke 4:16) and at least once even took a leading part in worship by reading the Scriptures (Luke 4:17). He often taught in the Temple and was concerned that the Temple truly be a house of prayer, not a marketplace (Luke 19:45–46).

Jesus taught something new about worship. Once a Samaritan woman asked him where it was best to worship—on the mountain where her ancestors had prayed or in Jerusalem. Jesus replied, "The hour is coming when you will worship the Father neither on this mountain nor in Jerusalem. . . . God is Spirit, and those who worship him must worship in Spirit and truth" (John 4:21–24).

What does this mean? It means that we now worship God in the Spirit and truth of Jesus, the Son of God. Although we do need places to worship, Jesus tells us that he himself is the primary place, the temple where God dwells. As he said on one occasion, "'Destroy this temple and in three days I will raise it up.' . . . He was speaking about the temple of his body" (John 2:19–21). Through the sacraments of initiation, we are incorporated into this new temple, this body of Christ. We are now the sign and sacrament of God's presence on earth.

Our worship of God in the body of Christ, in the Spirit and truth of Jesus, "is not tied exclusively to any one place. The whole earth is sacred" (*Catechism*, 1179). In this sense it is true that we do not need church buildings. But this is not the whole story.

After Jesus ascended into heaven, his disciples would gather on the first day of the week to keep his message alive and to celebrate his risen presence in the Eucharist. They needed a *place* to do this: a place to come together, to tell their stories, and to share their meal.

At first the early Christians met in one another's homes. Later, when assemblies grew larger and worship in public became more acceptable, they used Roman basilicas for their gatherings. A *basilica* was not a temple or a place of worship; rather, it was a building designed for public meetings and other business. Even later, when Christians began to design and build their own churches, they used the familiar basilica form as a model, often adapting it to the shape of a cross.

Many churches all over the world were built according to this model. The words *apse, nave,* and *narthex* are still used to describe these areas in a church building:

• *apse*: a semicircular domed area

• *nave*: a large open assembly area

• *narthex*: a lobby, porch, vestibule.

The House of God

Our parish church, the place where we gather to worship, is a visible sign of our faith. It is the place where God dwells, the tenting place of his eucharistic presence. It is not only a house for us, for the Church, but also God's house. Churches are not simply gathering places; they symbolize and "make visible the Church living in this place, the dwelling of God" with us in Christ (*Catechism*, 1180).

The parish church is a visible witness to the presence of Christ, who lives among his people: "Behold, God's dwelling is with the human race. He will dwell with them and they will be his people and God himself will always be with them" (Revelation 21:3).

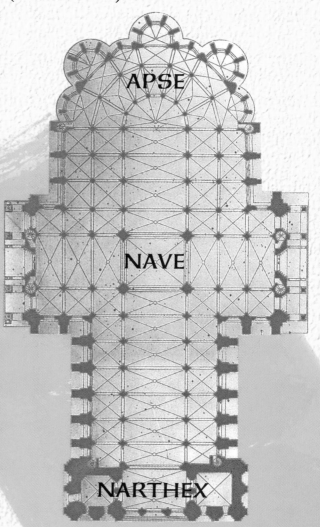

A Place of Celebration

Our parish church serves multiple purposes, but the most important is the celebration of the Eucharist. Earlier in this book, when we described the celebration of the Eucharist, we spoke of gathering, storytelling, meal sharing, and commissioning. In each of these aspects, how does the church building itself help us to celebrate the Eucharist? How does the design or shape of the church serve these four functions?

Gathering The church is the place where we gather for worship. We gather to do something together. This fact makes the design of a church different from the design of a sports stadium or a movie theater, for example. Most large public spaces have a stage where the action takes place and an area set aside for the spectators or audience. In church there is no stage because at Mass there is no audience. We are all *doers,* and the entire assembly area is the stage.

If we visit an empty church, the gathering area will look strange. The space only looks "right" when it is being used. Visiting an empty church is something like visiting an amusement park during the winter when it is closed. We can imagine what the park looks like with lights flashing, music playing, crowded with happy people. But the park needs actual people and real activity to look right. And the nave of the church needs a worshiping assembly of people to look right.

From wherever we stand in the assembly area, our attention is drawn to three important pieces of furniture: the presider's chair, the lectern, and the altar. The presider's chair is positioned so that the priest is seen to be both a member of the assembly and the leader of the assembly. In the principal church of a diocese, the chair (*cathedra* in Latin) for the bishop gives its name to the entire building, the *cathedral.*

Storytelling The church must be designed for the proclamation of God's word. We must be able to hear and see well. Good acoustics (sound quality) and sight lines are very important for this function.

The readings are proclaimed from the *lectern,* or *ambo,* a reading stand upon which the lectionary is placed and from which we proclaim the word of God.

It may be hard to believe, but originally Catholics worshiped standing. Even today the standing posture indicates that the worshiper is alert and ready to follow in the footsteps of Jesus. Standing is a mark of both reverence and readiness.

In the fifteenth century, as the readings and sermon became longer, Christians began to sit for the Liturgy of the Word. Pews and fixed seating began

Point out the altar, the presider's chair, and the lectern or ambo.

to be used in churches at about the time that the printing press was invented. People in church began to line up like lines on a printed page to hear the word of God read to them from a printed book.

Meal Sharing   As the liturgical action moves from storytelling to the sharing of our meal, our attention moves from the lectern to the altar. The altar is not an ordinary table. On the *altar* the sacrifice of the cross is made present under the sacramental signs. The altar is also the table of the Lord, to which we are all invited.

The altar, which is anointed with oil when a church is dedicated, also represents Christ, the Anointed One. As a sign of love for Christ, the priest greets the altar with an act of reverence at the beginning and end of the Eucharist.

In the thirteenth century Catholics did not receive Holy Communion frequently. Instead looking at the sacred Host after the consecration became the high point of the Mass. So Catholics began to kneel during the eucharistic prayer. As the practice of kneeling was extended, kneeling benches were introduced, often attached to the back of the chairs or pews.

Commissioning   Following Communion we are dismissed and commissioned to take the gospel message from the church to our daily lives in the world. What happens in the church must be connected to our lives outside the church. This connection is made clearer when the design and furnishings of the church building are related to the community it serves.

 Describe the many ways your parish church helps you to celebrate the liturgy.

CATHOLIC TEACHINGS

About Churches

The Eucharist not only remembers and makes present the past (the Last Supper) but it also makes present the future, our banquet with Christ in heaven. The church building that houses the Blessed Sacrament is a sign of this future banquet, the world to come. When we enter a church, we know that we are entering a very special, "heavenly" place, a symbol of the Father's house toward which we are journeying.

St. Mary's Cathedral, San Francisco

A Place of Worship

Because the sacrament of Baptism is the spiritual door to the Church, the baptismal font or baptismal pool is usually located near the front door when possible. In fact one early Church custom was to build the baptismal pool completely outside the church, in a separate building near the entrance. This building was called the *baptistry*. It signified the absolute need for Baptism before celebrating the Eucharist with the assembly. Today as we enter the doors of the church, we dip our fingers into blessed water and make the sign of the cross, that sign in which we were baptized. Each time we gather as the body of Christ for Eucharist, we continue and renew the celebration of our Baptism.

In this baptismal area you will also see a niche in the wall or a little chest called the *ambry*. It contains three vessels of oil: the oil of catechumens, which is used to bless and strengthen those preparing for baptism; the oil of the sick, with which the priest strengthens and heals those who are ill; and the sacred chrism, which is used in celebrating the sacraments of Baptism, Confirmation, and Holy Orders. The word *Christ* means "anointed one." So being anointed with oil is a sign of the special and strengthening presence of Christ, the Anointed One.

The reconciliation chapel, a small space designed for the celebration of the sacrament of Reconciliation (confession), is often located in the baptismal area. This reflects the historical connection between the sacraments of Baptism and Reconciliation. As we will see in Chapter 10, the sacrament of Penance or Reconciliation developed from the need of those Christians who had not been faithful to their baptismal promises and who had separated themselves from the community by grave sin.

Another important area of a Catholic church is the place set aside for the tabernacle. Sometimes this is a side chapel; sometimes it is a prominent place in the sanctuary. The *tabernacle* is the place in which the Eucharist is kept, or reserved. The word comes from the Latin for "tent" or "little house."

We have seen that Christ becomes present at the Eucharist in several ways. At different times during the eucharistic celebration, our attention is directed to these different ways in which Christ is really present: He is present in the gathered assembly and in the person of the priest.

He is present in the Scriptures. He is present most especially under the forms of bread and wine. And as we are commissioned to go out into the world, we find Christ present there also.

Christ is also present in the *Blessed Sacrament,* that is, in the Eucharist reserved in the tabernacle. The Blessed Sacrament is reserved in this way so that the eucharistic Bread may be taken to those who are sick and to those who are dying. In addition the tabernacle has become the focus for the adoration of Christ under the eucharistic species. Catholics have a long tradition of praying before the tabernacle.

The vestments worn by the priest at the liturgy have their roots in the earliest years of the Church. Originally they came from the way that ordinary people dressed. Today their function has changed. As powerful visible parts of our liturgy, they help us to celebrate the sacred mysteries of the Church. Like everything connected with the liturgy, vestments should be beautiful and well made because they are part of our worship of God.

Some churches are spacious enough to include a eucharistic chapel, a space especially designed for private prayer and adoration. This quiet place simply yet beautifully emphasizes and honors the real presence of Christ in the Blessed Sacrament.

A lamp or candle burning before the tabernacle indicates to Catholics that the consecrated Bread is present there. Candles will also be found in other devotional areas and in the assembly area of the Church. At every Mass candles are lit. Once they were used primarily to give light for reading the Scriptures and celebrating the sacred action. Now that churches are fitted with electric lighting, candles have lost much of their practical function. Yet their symbolic purpose remains.

The beautiful quality of candlelight reminds us of Christ, the Light of the World. As a candle consumes itself in the service of the liturgy, so must we in the service of God and of others. A candle is also a symbol of the continual presence of God to us and of us to God.

Find time this week to make a visit to the Blessed Sacrament. In your prayer tell Jesus anything that is on your mind or in your heart.

Seeing, Hearing, Doing

Like our homes, church buildings can tell us so much just by the way they look. In some older churches, for example, you may find many paintings, statues, mosaics, and perhaps even several altars. Modern churches do not have these. Why are there such differences?

In the early days of the liturgy, when Latin was the spoken language of the congregation, both the ear and the eye had something to do. The ear listened to the meaning of the words, and the eye followed the sacred action. As Latin became less and less understood by the people in the congregation, their ears had less to do. So churches began to be more elaborately decorated to become feasts for the eyes.

In the early Middle Ages, a greater stress began to be placed on the sacrificial dimension of the Eucharist, and Holy Communion was received only by the clergy. Therefore the altar was moved farther away from the faithful and was placed against the wall.

From early times this wall had been decorated with a painting of the cross, the Lamb of God, or Christ in glory. These paintings now began to be placed on the altar itself. The altar was filled with statues or paintings: first the crucifixion, then the patron saint of the parish or town. Later other saints were added.

Finding the Balance

After the Second Vatican Council (1962–65), the bishops determined that the liturgy would once again be celebrated in our own languages. Once again we can understand Sacred Scripture and the prayers at Mass. As our ears became active again, we discovered that sometimes too many decorations in the church could distract us from concentrating on what we were hearing! Today we Catholics are looking for a balance of seeing, hearing, and doing.

Does this mean that newer churches are better than the older ones? Does this mean that churches should have no decoration at all? No, absolutely not. We will not strengthen the ear by starving the eye. No one wants to remove statues and decorations from our churches simply to get rid of them. Statues and beautiful objects of art, banners, and flowers will always be an important part of the environment for our worship.

Many churches have stained-glass windows. In former times the pictures formed by the stained glass, in addition to bathing the assembly area with beautiful light, illustrated Bible stories for those who could not read. But stained-glass windows are not merely history lessons. Their artistic beauty reveals to us something of the beauty of God.

Around the walls of many churches, you will find the stations of the cross. This is a set of pictures, statues, or even simple crosses (numbered from one to fourteen) which mark incidents in the last journey of Jesus to the cross.

Scripture UPDATE

An image from the Bible that tells us about our union with Christ is that of a "building." Saint Peter told the first Christians, "Like living stones, let yourselves be built into a spiritual house to be a holy priesthood to offer spiritual sacrifices" (1 Peter 2:5). And in the preface for the dedication of a church we pray,

You continue to build your Church with
    chosen stones,
enlivened by the Spirit,
and cemented together by love.

What does it mean to you to be a "living stone"?

Chancery Chapel, Diocese of Victoria (Texas)

This form of devotional prayer became popular in the late Middle Ages. The desire of Christians to follow in the footsteps of Jesus on his way to the cross had led to a long tradition of pilgrimage to the Holy Land. Those who could not afford the expense of the long and dangerous trip to Jerusalem could, by praying the way of the cross, participate in the passion of Jesus in their own villages. Either individually or as a parish, we still pray the stations of the cross today, especially during Lent. We go to each station and meditate on an event of the passion. However, the church is primarily a place for our liturgical worship. Personal devotions, such as the stations of the cross, should not distract from the principal purpose of the assembly area.

There is a great variety in the way Catholic churches are decorated. Some have many statues; others have none. Some churches have marble altars and golden ceilings; others have simple wooden altars and plaster ceilings. When we visit the home of friends, we know that the warmth, hospitality, and friendship we experience there are more important than the cost or style of the furniture. In the same way, in a Catholic church the principal beauty is found in the hospitality of our assembly, our devotion to the Eucharist, and the love we carry forth to our brothers and sisters.

 Describe those things in your parish church that help you to pray.

PUTTING IT TOGETHER

things to think about

A church building is both God's house and a house for the Church, the people of God. Some Catholics expect God's house to be a place of silence. Other Catholics expect this gathering space, their house, to be a place where they can greet friends and encourage one another in the Lord. Can both these expectations be met in a way that is both reverent and prayerful?

things to share

Describe to three or four of your Catholic friends the most beautiful church you have ever seen. Ask them to do the same. What is it that makes these churches "beautiful"? Are the things that you selected as signs of a beautiful church the same elements that your friends picked?

WORDS TO REMEMBER

Find and define the following:

altar _____
_____
_____

tabernacle _____
_____
_____

OnLine WITH THE PARISH

How does your parish church building serve the four functions of our Eucharistic celebration? Do the areas for Baptism, Reconciliation, and reservation of the Eucharist match those described in this chapter?

Using simple materials, make a scale model of your parish church as it looks today. Can you find old photos and drawings of your parish church as it looked in previous decades or as it was being built?

What is the most important function of the church building?

1

Why is reverence shown to the altar at the beginning and at the end of the Eucharist?

2

Why is the baptismal font or pool usually located near the entrance to the church?

3

Give two reasons why Catholics reserve the Eucharist in the tabernacle.

4

Name some things in your parish church that help Catholics to pray.

5

Life in the Spirit

Think about your parish church. Then pray the following prayer slowly, and see what meaning it has for your life:

How lovely your dwelling,
   O LORD of hosts!
My soul yearns and pines
   for the courts of the LORD.
My heart and flesh cry out
   for the living God.
Psalm 84:2–3

You may want to illustrate this passage with several drawings or photos of your parish church, both inside and out. Make a poster or booklet to share with others in your group.

CHAPTER 8

Seasons of Praise

Every day I will bless you;
     I will praise your name forever.
Psalm 145:2

The seasons of the year move in a natural cycle—coming to life, growing, flowering, dying, being born again. Do you see this same cycle in your own life?

The Liturgical Seasons

Our life of prayer in the Church follows the same beautiful cycle of coming to life, growing, flowering, dying, being born again. Just as the seasons give variety to nature, the seasons of the liturgical year (the Church's year) give variety to the liturgy. Our life of prayer has its seasons also.

The two principal seasons of the liturgical year are formed around the two great feasts of Easter and Christmas. First we will explore the season of Easter and its preparation period, Lent. Then we will look at the season of Christmas and its preparation time, Advent. Finally we will explore Ordinary Time, the period between the Lent-Easter season and the Advent-Christmas season.

We can see a certain parallel with the birth, life, death cycle of the natural year. We can think of two great moments, birth and death, separated by the ongoing experiences of growing and changing. The Church year, then, has two main seasons, Lent-Easter and Advent-Christmas, separated by two seasons of Ordinary Time.

The seasons of the Church year do not exist simply for the sake of variety or change; they serve a much deeper purpose. As we have learned, each time we celebrate the liturgy, we celebrate the paschal mystery of Christ. In the liturgical year, the Church unfolds the entire mystery of Christ. This mystery is so complex and rich in meaning that no one single prayer or liturgical celebration can ever express it adequately.

For example, let's say that your mom or dad buys a car which you hope might be yours someday (now this takes some imagination!). You want to take a photograph of it to send to a friend. Where are you going to stand to take the picture? From the side, the picture won't show the lines of the hood and grille. If you stand in front, the picture won't show the fender wells. There is no way a flat piece of photographic film can fully capture the beauty of the three-dimensional object. Perhaps the best you can do is to walk around the car and take pictures from various angles and perspectives.

The liturgical year helps us to "walk around" the paschal mystery. During the course of a year, we view it from different angles, in different lights. Within the cycle of a year, the Church unfolds the whole mystery of Christ, from his incarnation and birth until his ascension, the day of Pentecost, and the expectation of his return in glory.

As we celebrate the mystery of Christ, we are not merely recalling past events. When we celebrate in memory of Jesus, our liturgical remembering (anamnesis) makes the mystery present.

The liturgy enables us to pass from our past-present-future concept of time into God's time of salvation, so that the grace and mystery of the event remembered are in some way made present. When we hear the passion of Christ proclaimed on Good Friday and sing "Were You There When They Crucified My Lord?" the answer is *yes*! You were there! You are there now! You do not have to feel disappointed that all the wonderful events of our faith happened long before you were born. These wonderful events of Christianity are happening now, *today*.

Before we look at the various seasons of the liturgical year, we will look at the word that gives us the key to understanding why we have a liturgical year in the first place. That word is *today*.

A prayer from the psalms that we often find in the liturgy is:

> Oh, that today you would hear his voice:
>   Do not harden your hearts.…
> Psalm 95:7–8

The liturgical year, with its various feasts and seasons, helps us to keep our hearts open *each day* to the voice of God in our lives and in our world.

Throughout the liturgical year we experience for ourselves what Saint Paul described: "Behold, now is a very acceptable time; behold, now is the day of salvation" (2 Corinthians 6:2). These wonderful events of Christianity are happening now, *today*.

The Lord's Day

When most Catholics think of the major feasts of the liturgical year, they usually think of Christmas and Easter. But the *original* Christian feast day is Sunday. Sunday is the key to the whole liturgical year.

At the time of Jesus, Sunday was called "the first day of the week." The other days were simply numbered in order: the second day, the third day, and so on. The only day given a special name was the seventh day, the Sabbath. Each of the four gospels mentions explicitly that the resurrection of Jesus took place on "the first day of the week"—that is, Sunday.

The name for Sunday came originally from the Romans, who gave each day of the week a name honoring either a heavenly body or one of the gods (for example *Sun*day for the sun). The early Christians renamed the first day of the week, the Sun's Day, and called it the Lord's Day. In English the day is still called "Sunday"; "the Lord's Day" is only used in the context of religion. In some other modern languages, however, the very name on the calendar is literally "the Lord's Day": *domenica* in Italian, *domingo* in Spanish. All of these come from the Latin word for "Lord," *dominus*. But whatever we name it, this day is our primary holy day because this day was chosen by God to transform history! This is the day Christ rose from the dead.

The Christian celebration of Sunday has a different focus from the Jewish sabbath. Jews rest on the sabbath because God rested on the seventh day: "God blessed the seventh day and made it holy, because on it he rested from all the work he had done in creation" (Genesis 2:3). The Christian Sunday is primarily a day to assemble for worship. At first the Christian Sunday was a workday like the other days of the week; only later did it take on the Jewish characteristic of a day of rest.

The Sunday assembly for Eucharist is at the very heart of the meaning of Sunday. As we sit at the eucharistic table—with Jesus, with the disciples, with all those who believed in the resurrection throughout ages past, and with all those who will

believe in ages to come—past, present, and future become one. We come to the table of the One who died in the past and taste the future banquet of heaven. We sing of our confidence in life:

> Dying you destroyed our death,
> rising you restored our life.

We sing of our freedom:

> Lord, by your cross and resurrection
> you have set us free.

 In which eucharistic acclamation do we proclaim our faith that Christ will come again?

Day of Resurrection

What we think about Sunday depends on what we think about the resurrection. Do you believe in the resurrection? You will surely answer yes to that question. But what if we ask, "Do you believe in the resurrection not only as a historical event but also as happening *now*?"

What does it mean to believe that the resurrection is now? Consider this: Have you ever watched the tape of a sporting event on television already knowing that your favorite team had won the game? Knowing the ending can take the excitement out of a ball game, but it can certainly give you confidence and hope at those times when your team seems to be losing. Or have you ever watched a movie that you have seen before? In spite of all the twists and turns of plot, you already know that everything turns out all right in the end. In the same way, the resurrection tells us that everything will turn out more than "all right" for us. The resurrection tells us that sorrow will be overwhelmed by joy, loss by victory, and death by new life. This is the role the resurrection of Jesus plays in our daily lives.

There are times when life can be discouraging and the world disappointing. There are times when we look around us and see so much pain and violence that we are tempted to wonder: Is death winning the battle? But in the midst of all that is evil in the world, the resurrection is God's great cry of triumph. The resurrection is our proof that life has a happy ending. The risen Jesus is our proof that loving and forgiving one another even as God loves and forgives us is a road that leads, not to death, but to life. The resurrection lets us know that God is in charge. Sin and evil will never win in the end. God's love and God's life will triumph.

CHRIST HAS DIED · CHRIST HAS RISEN · CHRIST WILL COME AGAIN

CATHOLIC TEACHINGS

About Sunday

The teaching of the Church is clear. The most important way Catholics praise God and honor the risen Christ is by participating in the Eucharist, our source of strength and joy. This is the obligation of every Catholic. This means that, except for a serious reason, we must worship God at the liturgy. Another way to celebrate Sunday is to share strength and joy with others through visiting the sick, the infirm, and the elderly. Our Sunday celebration can be enriched by spending time with our families and by setting aside extra quiet time for prayer and reading.

Spending leisure time well is important for everyone. "Traditional activities (sports, restaurants, etc.), and social necessities (public services, etc.), require some people to work on Sundays, but everyone should still take care to set aside sufficient time for leisure" (*Catechism*, 2187).

The Lenten Retreat

You probably already know a lot about the liturgical season of Lent. *Lent* is the time of preparation for the celebration of Easter. It begins on Ash Wednesday and extends to Holy Thursday. Lent is like a retreat. It is a time of prayer, fasting, and almsgiving (which means sharing what we have with the poor).

When you hear the word *Lent,* what picture comes to mind? Penance, purple, fish, ashes, fasting, sacrifice, giving up movies? These are the images many Catholics associate with Lent. But your idea of Lent will be closer to the Church's meaning of the season if the first thing that comes to your mind is an image of new life—of Baptism. Baptism provides the key to Lent.

We have seen that in the fourth and fifth centuries, the Church developed liturgies to assist people who wanted to become Christians. The final forty days of this faith journey, the final "forty-day retreat" before Baptism, became what we now call Lent. Lent is the time for the catechumens to continue their preparation for Baptism, Confirmation and Eucharist. It is a time for those of us who are already baptized to reaffirm what this sacrament means in our lives today.

When was the last time you thought about your Baptism? For some Christians, Baptism is an event that happened long ago and does not have much impact on what they do today. But Baptism, as we have seen, changes us so radically that we are different, "marked" forever. Baptism gives us the spiritual mark that we call *character.* We are "characterized" by the life of Jesus that we find in the gospels. Once we are baptized, the promises of our Baptism should influence our decisions for the rest of our lives.

When we understand Baptism as the focus of Lent, the things we choose to give up can be more clearly understood. We saw that the ritual sacrifices in the Old Testament found their meaning in joyful union with God, not simply in the death of an animal or the destruction of something. Similarly our Lenten sacrifices are not a negative giving up of something. Rather, they direct us to a positive goal, joyful union with God.

Dying and Rising

Baptism is both a dying and a rising. Saint Paul says, "If, then, we have died with Christ, we believe that we shall also live with him" (Romans 6:8). The penitential aspect of Lent, the "giving something up" part, is related to the dying aspect of Baptism. But the "dying" is not an end in itself. We need to keep our eyes fixed on the "rising" that Baptism offers us.

But death, in whatever form it comes, is never easy. Sometimes we resist change in our lives, even change for the better. Jesus promises us that life will spring out of death: "Unless a grain of wheat falls to the ground and dies, it remains just a grain of wheat; but if it dies, it produces much fruit" (John 12:24). The intention of the farmer is not to kill the seed. Yet in order to grow, the seed must change its life-form. It cannot remain the same old seed!

Here is another example. When you were in the first grade, you were at the bottom of the heap; everybody else was older and seemed stronger and smarter. They could write cursive, multiply, and knew the capitals of all fifty states. Now, however, you are older and stronger and smarter. But just when it seems that you are at the top, it is time for you to move on. You have to start over again in high school, and once again everyone else is older and stronger and smarter.

What if you would decide that you don't want to give up being at the top of the heap, that you want to stay where you are, where you are comfortable? You would probably be told, "Give it up! Move on!"

Sometimes we get attached to something that keeps us from moving on. We can get caught at a particular stage of growth in our Christian lives. But during Lent we may hear the voice of the Spirit tell us, "Give it up! Move on!"

The moving on does not have to be a big thing. Rather, it is like the seed that needs to be planted—something good in it self, but only in its proper time. For most of us, moving on involves letting go of something *good* in order to get *an even greater good*. It means planting small seeds and looking forward to a good harvest.

 Is there something now that keeps you from moving on in your faith? Write about it in your journal.

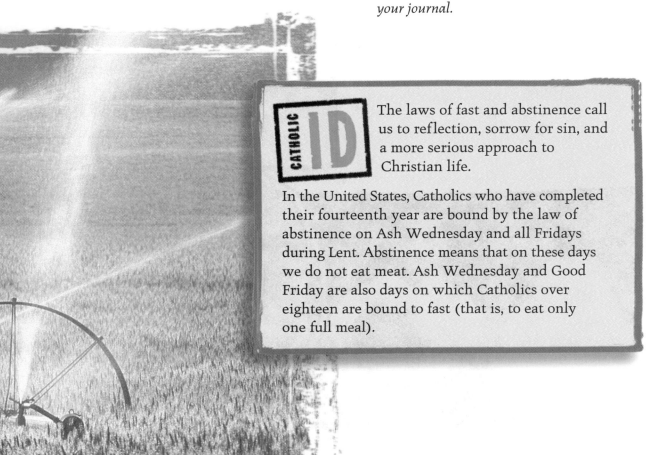

The Triduum

Did you know that the oldest Christian feast is Sunday? Jesus rose on the Sunday after the Passover, and, remembering this, Christians began to celebrate the Sunday closest to the Jewish Passover with special solemnity. This "Christian Passover" became what we now call Easter.

The Christian Passover soon became the special time to celebrate the sacrament of Baptism, the sacrament of our passing over from death to life in Christ. As the rites and celebrations surrounding Christian initiation grew and developed, the Christian community found that one twenty-four-hour day was simply not enough time to experience the mystery, and the celebration was extended to three days. Today we call this celebration the *Triduum,* from the Latin word meaning "three days."

The Triduum took hundreds of years to develop into the three-day celebration we know today. Saint Augustine speaks of the Triduum of Christ crucified, buried, and risen. In Augustine's time the Triduum was Good Friday, Holy Saturday, and Easter Sunday. About two hundred years later, an evening Liturgy of the Lord's Supper became a part of the Holy Thursday celebration in Rome. The Triduum was then extended to include not only Friday but also the evening before Friday. The three-day observance now begins with the Mass of the Lord's Supper in the evening on Holy Thursday and ends with evening prayer on Easter Sunday.

The solemn liturgies of the Triduum are the most important liturgies of the Church year. The washing of the feet after the gospel of Holy Thursday is followed by the reading of the Passion and the adoration of the cross on Good Friday. At the Easter Vigil, the darkness and grief of Good Friday is broken by the blessing of the new fire and the paschal candle, the singing of the Easter Proclamation, the first sounds of the "Alleluia," and the sacramental initation of the catechumens.

These are ceremonies we can experience at no other time during the year. As we participate in them each year, they teach us the meaning of Christ's life, death, and resurrection, not in words alone, but in symbols and rituals: in fire, in water, in darkness, in light, in walking, in kneeling, in standing again. Describing these ceremonies or reading about them can never equal being there.

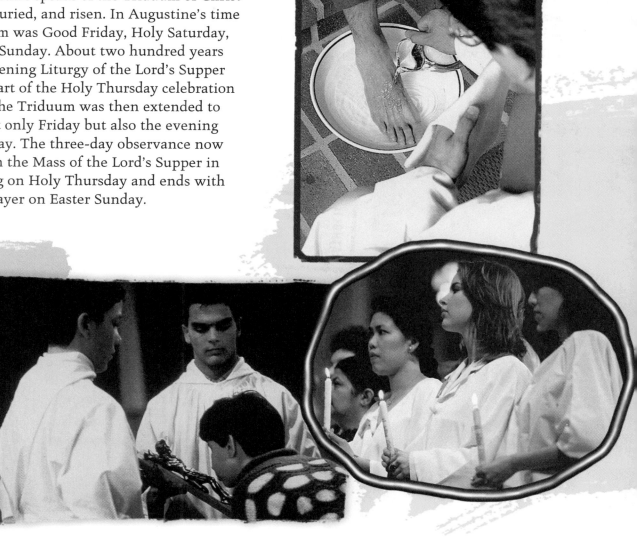

Preparing for Easter

It takes a special kind of attention and alertness to enter into these mysteries. How can we come to these events fully aware and prepared? The Church recommends that we fast, especially on Good Friday and, where possible, Holy Saturday as well. This fasting is very different from dieting. The purpose of fasting is not to lose weight; its purpose is to gain insight into the mysteries of the Triduum. It is a fast of awareness. It creates a hunger that can be satisfied only by the best of foods: our Easter Eucharist, which we share with those who join us at our eucharistic table for the very first time.

Catholics eighteen years of age and under are not obliged to fast, but even younger Catholics can prepare, through prayer and simple acts of love and selflessness, to celebrate the Triduum with an open heart and a clear mind. If we have prepared well, as we stand at the foot of the cross on Good Friday and look up at Jesus dying for us, all our doubts and questions—Why did my baby sister die? Why did my parents have to get divorced? Why does my dad drink so much? Why didn't our team win? Why don't I have more friends?—fade into one question. We simply ask, "Jesus, how much do you love me?" And he stretches wide his arms on the cross and answers, "This much."

As a group, plan ways you will prepare during Lent this year to celebrate the Triduum together in your parish.

Scripture UPDATE

A scriptural theme that can be followed throughout the Triduum is the symbol of the Lamb of God. On Holy Thursday the reading recalls the Passover lamb (Exodus 12: 1–8). On Good Friday Isaiah describes "the suffering servant" who is compared to a lamb (Isaiah 53:7). At the Easter Vigil the proclamation reminds us:

> This is our passover feast,
> when Christ, the true Lamb, is slain. . . .

On Easter Sunday this triumphant song praises the victorious Lamb:

> A Lamb the sheep redeems: Christ,
> who only is sinless,
> Reconciles sinners to the Father.

things to think about

What do you and your family do to make Sunday different from the other days of the week? In what practical ways do you abstain from work and other concerns that would keep you from praying and relaxing on the Lord's Day?

What happens if work is necessary on Sunday? If this is the case in your family, how do you celebrate Sunday? How does your family pray and relax?

things to share

With several of your friends, think up ways in which you could "help Lent happen" in your home, perhaps in your room. For example, Lent is Baptism time. What reminders of Baptism do you have around the house? Do you still have the candle you received at your baptism? Water is a primary symbol of Baptism: Where there is no water, we have a desert. Remember that violet is the liturgical color for Lent. How can you use these symbols?

WORDS TO REMEMBER

Find and define the following:

Lent _____

_____

_____

Triduum _____

_____

_____

OnLine WITH THE PARISH

The liturgical year is a construct; it has to be "made." Often, at the change of the liturgical seasons, there is a lot of work to be done in your parish church in order to enable the liturgical season to come alive for the parishioners. These are especially good times to volunteer your services to help clean and decorate the church for Lent, the Triduum, Advent, or Christmas.

Why do Christians keep *Sunday* holy?

1

How does the resurrection of Jesus help us in the difficult times of our lives?

2

What does it mean to say that Baptism changes us radically?

3

What do the solemn liturgies of the Triduum teach us?

4

What do we mean by the liturgical "today"?

5

Life in the Spirit

This week listen carefully to the opening prayer of the Sunday Eucharist. It can be found in the sacramentary or in the missalette. Make it your prayer for the week. This is the alternative opening prayer for the Eighteenth Sunday in Ordinary Time:

God our Father,
gifts without measure flow from your goodness
to bring us your peace.
Our life is your gift.
Guide our life's journey,
for only your love makes us whole.
Keep us strong in your love.

We ask this through Christ our Lord.

A Year of Glory

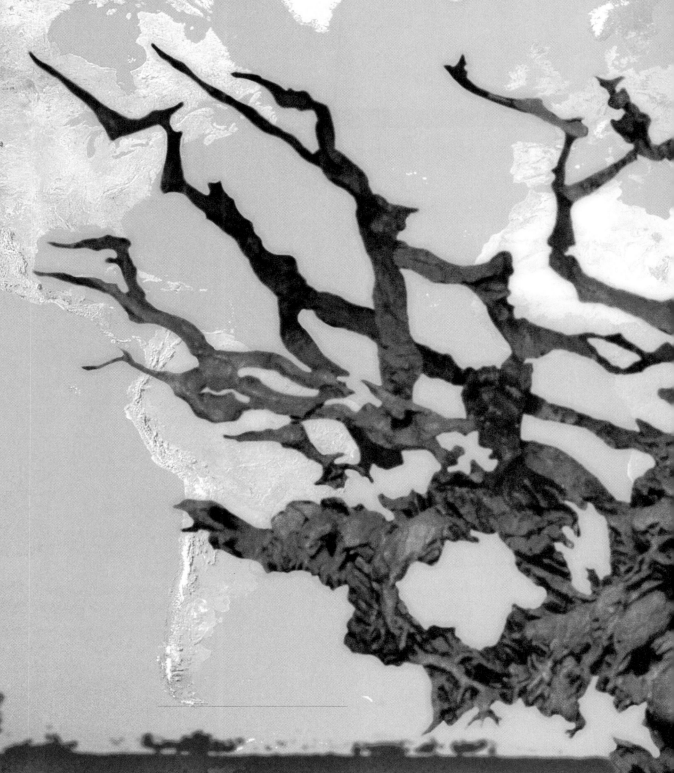

Praise the LORD, all you nations!
Give glory, all you peoples!
The LORD's love for us is strong;
the LORD is faithful forever.
Hallelujah!

Psalm 117

"There is a season, turn, turn, turn . . .
And a time for every purpose under heaven."©
(Song lyrics adapted from Ecclesiastes 3:1)

How do these words suggest
that we live in a world of time, of
change, of new beginnings?

The Great Fifty Days

We human beings need change. Yet we often
don't like sudden changes. We like predictable
changes. Usually we like to know ahead of time
that a change is coming so that we can prepare
for it. The seasons of the Church year are seasons
of change and seasons of preparation.

That's what Lent does—it prepares us for the great
events of the Triduum. Now we will follow this
great event to its fulfillment in the Easter season
and at Pentecost.

At the heart of our Christian life is the belief that God has radically changed the universe through the paschal mystery of Jesus. We call this radical change *salvation.* It is the focus of our Easter celebration.

Easter, after all, is not just one more feast among others. Easter is "'the Feast of feasts,' the 'Solemnity of solemnities'" (*Catechism,* 1169). Easter is so important that we cannot even begin to celebrate it adequately in one day. It takes a week—and even more; it takes a "week of weeks." It takes fifty days, a *Pentecost* (from the Greek word meaning "fifty"). *Each day* of these fifty days is Easter.

At the Easter Vigil we received new members into our community through the sacraments of initiation. During their time of preparation, the catechumens learned about the sacraments "from outside," as it were. Now, as *neophytes* (newly initiated Christians), they experience the sacraments of Baptism and Eucharist "from within" the community.

For the neophytes (and for us as well) this fifty-day season of Easter is the time of mystagogy. *Mystagogy* is a time for learning about and reflecting on the mysteries of faith. The Easter season is a time for the community and the neophytes to grow in their understanding of the paschal mystery. It is a time to make the paschal mystery part of our lives through meditation on the gospel, sharing in the Eucharist, and doing good works.

Mystagogy is something like the process of being adopted. Imagine this: You have just been adopted into a new family. One day your new parents say, "Now that you're a member of the family, we want to tell you more about us and what you've gotten yourself into! Let's look at some family pictures together." So you look at pictures of grandparents, of aunts, uncles, and cousins. You discover that *your* picture will soon be in the album, too. You are now part of a whole family history and family system.

So it is with the newly baptized. They have not only "put on Christ"; they have also put on his body, the Church. They have joined a new family. And they (and we) take time during these fifty days to learn who that family, that Church, is. We find the picture of the birth and early growth of the Church in the Acts of the Apostles.

The Story Continues

The Acts of the Apostles forms one story with the Gospel of Luke. If you compare the way the two parts of this story (Luke 1:1–4 and Acts 1:1–2) begin, it is clear that Luke/Acts is meant to be read as a unit. Luke/Acts is a very special form of writing. The author wants to show three things: (1) the life and deeds of Jesus, (2) how his life and deeds were continued in the lives and deeds of the first disciples, and (3) how his life and deeds are to be continued by us in the Church today.

In Luke's Gospel we see Jesus healing the sick; in Acts we see Peter doing the same. In the gospel we see Jesus brought before the high priest to be interrogated; in Acts we see the same thing happening to Peter. The death of Stephen, the first martyr, parallels the death of Jesus. Stephen prays, "Lord, do not hold this sin against them" (Acts 7:60) as Jesus had prayed "Father, forgive them, they know not what they do" (Luke 23:34).

Why did Luke write in this way? He wanted to show us that what Jesus did during his lifetime, the first disciples also did during theirs, and we—today's disciples—are to do during ours! As we hear readings from the Acts of the Apostles proclaimed at each Mass during the great fifty days, we might ask ourselves these questions: "Is this our Church family today?" "Are we a healing Church?" "Are we a forgiving Church?" The stories in Acts are not simply stories of long-ago people and places, not simply faded pictures in some unknown photo album. They are *our* stories, *our* pictures. The challenge of the great fifty days of Easter is to continue the story of Luke/Acts today, in our Church and in our lives.

The First Pentecost

On the final day of our fifty-day celebration of Easter, we celebrate Pentecost. As with each feast and each liturgical season of the year, its meaning is best understood by looking at the Scripture readings. The readings for Pentecost speak of the sending of the Holy Spirit. The word *spirit* is a translation of the Hebrew word *ruah,* which means "breath," "air," or "wind."

In the second reading for Pentecost, we read about the descent of the Holy Spirit upon the disciples: As they were gathered together, they heard a noise like a strong wind (*ruah*). "Then there appeared to them tongues as of fire. . . . And they were all filled with the holy Spirit and began to speak in different tongues, as the Spirit enabled them to proclaim" (Acts 2:3–4). Right away we begin to see the gifts and graces of the Spirit at work in the Church.

In the gospel for Pentecost, we read John's account of Jesus giving the Holy Spirit. On the evening of the first day of the week, "Jesus came and stood in their midst and said to them, 'Peace be with you. . . . As the Father has sent me, so I send you.' And. . . . he breathed [*ruah*] on them and said to them, 'Receive the holy Spirit'" (John 20:19–22). Sins are to be forgiven! The gifts of peace and reconciliation are given to the Church.

We do not need to ask *when* the Holy Spirit is given: on Pentecost (as in Luke), on Easter Sunday (as in John), or on Good Friday when Jesus bowed his head and "handed over the spirit" (John 19:30). The liturgy is not concerned with retelling the past. The liturgy combines all these accounts in order that we might reflect and ask ourselves: "How does the Holy Spirit act in the Church today?" "How does the Spirit come to me?" The liturgy makes Pentecost present to us now, today.

Our understanding of the work of the Holy Spirit today comes from three sources. The first is the witness of the Scriptures, which we have briefly explored. The second is the public prayer of the Church, the liturgy. The third is our own lives and experience.

Pentecost Today

Let us consider the prayer of the Church. In Eucharistic Prayer IV we speak directly to God and recall Jesus' sending us the Holy Spirit:

> And that we might live no longer for ourselves
>   but for him,
> he sent the Holy Spirit from you, Father,
> as his first gift to those who believe,
> to complete his work on earth
> and bring us the fullness of grace.

What can we learn from this prayer? First we learn that the Holy Spirit is not the possession of an exceptional few. The Holy Spirit is given to *every* Christian, to all who believe. "First gift" does not mean that we first believe in Jesus and then the Holy Spirit is given to us as a reward for our good act. No, the Holy Spirit is God's free gift, given before any good work of ours.

We also learn here that the gift of the Holy Spirit is a gift of *mission*. When Jesus gave the Holy Spirit, he told the disciples, "As the Father has sent me, so I send you" (John 20:21). What the Father gave Jesus to do, the risen Lord commissions us to continue. This is the message of Pentecost. This is the work of the Holy Spirit. This is the work of a lifetime.

The Holy Spirit works with each one of us for the good of all. How is the Spirit breathing life into you?

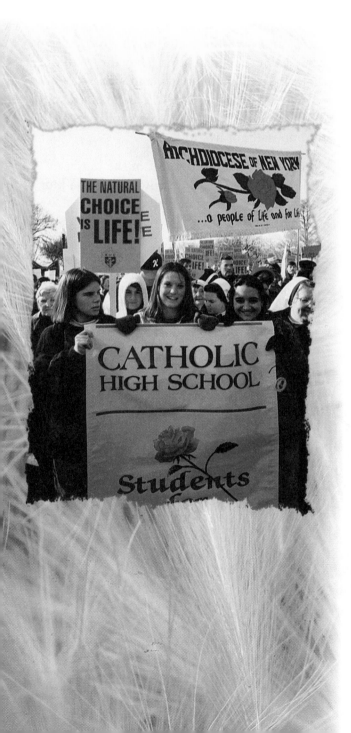

Scripture UPDATE

The Holy Spirit equips us for our mission by giving us seven gifts or *charisms*. The gifts of the Holy Spirit are wisdom, understanding, right judgment, courage, knowledge, reverence, and wonder and awe in the presence of the Lord. The source of these traditional names is Isaiah 11:2–3.

The gifts of the Spirit do not work automatically, of course. It is up to us to develop these gifts and to use them for our own spiritual growth and for the service of God and others.

Advent and Christmas

During World War II, when the United States and Japan were at war, the Japanese took over the Philippines. American missionaries working there were sent to prisoner-of-war camps. In one camp the guards allowed their prisoners to gather for prayer. Every day during the Lenten and Easter seasons, they prayed before a crucifix hung on the wall. When Advent came, they set up a small manger scene. On Christmas Day the figure of the infant Jesus was placed in the manger. One day a sister was praying at the manger scene. A Japanese guard posted nearby pointed first to the crucifix, then to the figure of the baby. "Same one?" he asked her. "Yes," she replied. "The same One." The guard's face saddened. "I am sorry," he said.

During Advent we go back to the beginning. We do not forget that we are celebrating the same Jesus who died and rose for us but we remember also that he chose to share ordinary human life with us. He chose to become one of us and to experience life as we do: its joys, sorrows, disappointments, hopes. He is indeed "the same One."

Advent is a time of joyful expectation. Joyful expectation! What do we expect, and why are we joyful? The answer to these questions is given in the Scriptures proposed for the season.

From the First Sunday of Advent until December 16, the readings express the hope and longing for that day when the plan of God will be completed. We dream of how things ought to be and long for the day when Christ will come again in glory. From December 17 to December 24, the readings direct our attention to the birth of Jesus.

The prophet Isaiah sets the tone for Advent. He voices the hope and longing of God's people, wandering far away from home, in exile in a foreign land. They want to return home. They dream of the day when God's rule will prevail and wars will end. God's people long for the time when all hatred and prejudice will cease, when the streets will be safe and children will not live in fear:

> Then the wolf shall be a guest of the lamb,
>   and the leopard shall lie down with the kid;
> The calf and the young lion shall browse
>   together,
>   with a little child to guide them.
> Isaiah 11:6

The Kingdom Among Us

How and when will this all come about? We do not know. Asked by the Pharisees when God's reign would come, Jesus replied, "The coming of the kingdom of God cannot be observed, and no one will announce, 'Look, here it is,' or, 'There it is.' For behold, the kingdom of God is among you" (Luke 17:20–21).

Madonna of the Streets, Raphael, 1514

Christmas is the season when we pray fervently for the final revelation of God's mysterious plan. We pray for an end to war, hunger, and injustice. We pray, *Marana tha!* "Come, Lord Jesus!"

Have you ever noticed how often at Mass we pray for the coming of Christ? Can you recall a few examples?

Although we pray for Christ to come again, Christmas teaches us to live in the present. Our attention is not fixed on a baby's birth long ago, nor does fear of the end of the world keep us awake at night. Christ comes now. The Spirit of Jesus is offered to us always, in the events of each day. It is in the present that we find Jesus, not yesterday, nor tomorrow, but today.

How can the kingdom be among us when the world is so full of sin and violence? To see the kingdom, we need a special kind of light: faith. The light of Advent (as symbolized in the Advent wreath and in all the other beautiful lights we see at this time of year) little by little replaces the darkness of doubt and discouragement. By the light of faith, we see the kingdom.

Christmas, then, is a celebration of light—the light of Christ, the Word made flesh. In the birth of Jesus, the invisible God becomes visible. In the life of Jesus, we see God's plan for the world unfold. This plan is revealed gently and quietly, even as God gently and quietly appeared among us in the stable at Bethlehem.

In our lives, too, God's plan is usually revealed gently and quietly: in a quiet moment of prayer, in the stillness after the loss of a friend, in those minutes at night before we fall asleep. Little by little we are to grow into the likeness of Christ. "Only when Christ is formed in us will the mystery of Christmas be fulfilled in us" (*Catechism*, 526).

CATHOLIC TEACHINGS

About Angels

Angels appear often in the stories we hear during the Advent and Christmas seasons. What does the Church believe about angels? We believe that angels are spirits created by God to be his servants and messengers. Angels assure us that God is concerned about us. Even their names speak of God: *Gabriel* means "strength of God," *Raphael* means "God's healing," and *Michael* means, "Who is like God?"

The whole Church benefits from the help of the angels, and each of us here on earth has an angel "as protector and shepherd" to guide us on the path of life (*Catechism*, 334, 336).

Ordinary Time

What is Ordinary Time? If we take *ordinary* to mean "usual, average, of inferior quality or second-rate," it will be hard to get excited about Ordinary Time. However, these days are not ordinary in that sense. *Ordinary* here means "not seasonal." *Ordinary Time* is the time that lies outside the seasons of Lent-Easter and Advent-Christmas. In Ordinary Time, the Church celebrates the mystery of Christ not in one specific aspect but in all its aspects.

During the *seasons* of the Church year, the readings from Scripture are chosen according to the theme of the season: Lent, Baptism; Easter, resurrection; the great fifty days of Easter, Acts of the Apostles; Advent, Isaiah and joyful expectation; Christmas, God's taking flesh. During Ordinary Time the readings are not chosen according to a theme. Rather, in Ordinary Time we read from the various books of the Bible from beginning to end in a continuous fashion. This is the key to understanding Ordinary Time.

Christ prayed that the Holy Spirit would enable us to carry on the work that the Father gave him. In order to do this, in order to carry on the work of Christ, we must know Christ. To know Christ, we must know the Scriptures, for, as Saint Jerome said, "Ignorance of the Scriptures is ignorance of Christ."

In Ordinary Time we concentrate for an entire year on the life and work of Jesus Christ as proclaimed in one of the Gospels, either Matthew, Mark, or Luke. (John's Gospel is read principally during the liturgical seasons.) As we meet Christ in the Scriptures, we come to know him better. Knowledge of the Scriptures is knowledge of Christ.

Everyday Growth

Ordinary Time enables us to hear the whole gospel—not just the "big stories" of birth, death, and resurrection, but all the "in between" stories, parables, and teachings. Our Christian life is not just Christmas and Easter. It is all the days in between, the ordinary days. And perhaps that is what makes it difficult.

We all enjoy the wonderful and the spectacular, the miraculous and the exceptional. Yet when we look around us and see people who have accomplished great things, we seldom find that these accomplishments occurred overnight. Think of the hours and years of practice that go into becoming an accomplished musician or a fluent translator or a computer expert. Obviously these skills were not acquired overnight.

The hardest part of following Jesus is simply that, for the most part, it is so terribly ordinary! Getting up every morning and going to school, treating others with respect and fairness, doing homework and chores every night, practicing a musical instrument day after day, showing up for sports practice night after night—these things seem so ordinary, so routine, and possibly even boring. However, we know that the truly valuable things in our lives are achieved just that way: little by little, day after day.

In a parable Jesus told the disciples that the kingdom of heaven is like a farmer who went out to sow his seed. As the farmer scattered the seed, some "fell on the path, and the birds came and ate it up. Other seed fell on rocky ground where it had little soil. It sprang up at once because the soil was not deep. And when the sun rose, it was scorched and it withered for lack of roots. Some seed fell among thorns, and the thorns grew up and choked it and it produced no grain. And some seed fell on rich soil and produced fruit. It came up and grew and yielded thirty, sixty, and a hundredfold" (Mark 4:4–8).

Scholars who know about such things tell us that at the time of Jesus, a return of a hundredfold was not an exceptional harvest. It is only an average-to-good harvest. Jesus tells us that the harvest is "ordinary." For the most part God is not revealed in the spectacular or the sensational. Rather, the miracle of the kingdom is found in our daily efforts and everyday growth. We take up our cross daily and allow God's Spirit to help us grow gradually into the likeness of Jesus.

 What does Ordinary Time of the Church year teach us about our lives?

 White, red, green, violet—what do these liturgical colors mean? Red (the color of fire) symbolizes the Holy Spirit, and is used on Pentecost and for the sacrament of Confirmation. Red (the color of blood) is also used on days when we celebrate the passion of Jesus (on Passion Sunday and Good Friday) and on the feasts of martyrs. White, the color of joy and victory, is used for the other feasts of the Lord, Mary, and the other saints. White is also used for the seasons of Easter and Christmas. Violet is used for the seasons of Lent and Advent. Green, the color of life and hope, is used during Ordinary Time.

PUTTING IT TOGETHER

things
to think about

Many people used to wait until Christmas Eve to decorate their trees. And Christmas parties were held after Christmas rather than during Advent. Would you want your family to keep these customs? Is the liturgy out of sync with the real world? What are the pros and cons of waiting for Christmas to celebrate Christmas?

things
to share

The seasons of life happen "naturally," but the seasons of the Church year need our help. How can you "help Advent happen" in your home? A symbol that many families use is the Advent wreath. The circle, the evergreen branches, the increasing light each week—each of these symbols reflects the themes of Advent. Do you keep this custom in your home? Ask several of your friends if they do. How is the wreath used? Who lights it? What prayers are said?

WORDS TO REMEMBER

Find and define the following:

neophyte _____

_____

_____

mystagogy _____

_____

_____

OnLine
WITH THE PARISH

How can you help your parish celebrate Advent and Christmas? By cleaning and decorating the church? By joining the youth choir? By helping with a parish action for the poor? Lend your time and talents!

What are the "great fifty days"? Be sure to mention when they begin and end.

1

What three things does the author of Luke/Acts wish to teach us?

2

In what symbolic way did the Spirit come upon the disciples at Pentecost?

3

In what way is Christmas a celebration of the kingdom among us?

4

What does Ordinary Time teach us about following Jesus?

5

Life in the Spirit

Whatever the liturgical season, music can be a powerful way to experience it. The tradition of Gregorian chant in worship and prayer is a long and rich one in the Church. Gospel music, classical music, folk music, songs in native languages, contemporary hymns—all can help us in giving glory to God.

What kind of liturgical music expresses your life in the Spirit? This week try listening to a style of liturgical music you may not be too familiar with. Does it help you give God glory? It was Saint Augustine who told us that the one who sings prays twice!

CHAPTER 10

The Sacrament of Reconciliation

Lord, you are kind and forgiving,
most loving to all who call on you.

Psalm 86:5

Some people were shocked when they learned that Pope John Paul II had gone to the jail cell of the man who tried to assassinate him. They were even more shocked when they found out that the pope forgave the man. Why do you think the pope did this? Are forgiveness and mercy so important in our lives?

Christ and the Samaritan Woman at the Well, Paolo Veronese, sixteenth century

Rich in Mercy

When the writers of Sacred Scripture wanted to describe their experience of God's love and mercy, they used some very dramatic imagery. The prophet Micah, for example, said that God "will cast into the depths of the sea all our sins" (Micah 7:19). When God forgives and removes our sins, he is described as putting them "as far as the east is from the west" (Psalm 103:12). Our God is truly a God of compassion!

Jesus knew this and wanted us to experience this forgiveness of God even more in our lives. Only God can forgive sins, and this is why Jesus, God's only Son, came among us. He wanted to free us from sin, to heal our wounded and broken natures. Who else but Jesus told the stories of the lost sheep and the prodigal son (Luke 15:1–7, 11–32)? He wanted us to know how much God loves us.

After Christ's resurrection the early Church community recognized what he had done for them. By offering his life for us on the cross, Jesus had redeemed us. He had reconciled us to God and to one another. This means that in Christ we were brought back into friendship again with God. We first share in this reconciliation and forgiveness at Baptism. But our rebirth in the waters of Baptism does not mean that we will never sin again. As we struggle to live a life of holiness, we do sin.

For this reason we need to be healed again. We need to turn to Jesus, who is really the sacrament of God's forgiveness. How do we do this? Jesus entrusted his Church with the mission of healing and forgiveness, especially in the sacraments. In the Eucharist we share in Christ's Body and Blood, given for us and shed for the forgiveness of sins. In the Eucharist we realize and share in the peace Christ gave to us.

Jesus did not stop there, however. He gave to his apostles and their successors the power to forgive sins. On Easter night Jesus appeared to his apostles and breathed on them. He said, "Receive the holy Spirit. Whose sins you forgive are forgiven them, and whose sins you retain are retained" (John 20:22–23). This same Holy Spirit makes our hearts ready to receive God's forgiveness. And we do this in a most wonderful way in a special sacrament.

Actually we may know this sacrament by many names. We call it the *sacrament of Reconciliation* because through it our relationship to God and to the community of the Church is restored. The sacrament is also called the sacrament of *Penance*. We have seen how penance (conversion, turning around) is our lifelong task. The sacrament of Penance celebrates our continuing conversion, our turning from selfishness and sin to the Spirit of love and generosity. The word *penance* can also mean that part of the sacrament in which the priest asks us to say certain prayers or to perform some other action to help atone for our sins.

Church documents usually call the sacrament *Penance* and those going to the sacrament *penitents*. For many years most Catholics called the sacrament *Confession. Confession*, however, names only one part of the sacrament and not the most important part at that. *Reconciliation* names what is most important, what Jesus does. Sinners are brought back to God and to the community. They are reconciled. The *sacrament of Reconciliation* is the name used in the rite itself.

The sacrament of Reconciliation is a beautiful celebration of love and forgiveness. It is sad that few people take the time to understand what it really offers us. The sacrament is never meant to make us feel false guilt or to become overly concerned with sin. Nor is the sacrament meant to make us blame ourselves for things beyond our control. The Church teaches us that it is meant for healing what is broken, for setting free that which is bound up. In addition this sacrament is not just intended for the times when we commit serious, or mortal, sin. Whenever we confess our venial sins, we are strengthened and grow in God's grace.

Only when we are more mature, perhaps, can we grow in our appreciation of what is really happening in this special sacramental moment. Let's look more closely at Reconciliation, part of its fascinating history, and its celebration in the life of the Church. Let's experience in a deeper way why this sacrament is not something to be feared but something in which to rejoice.

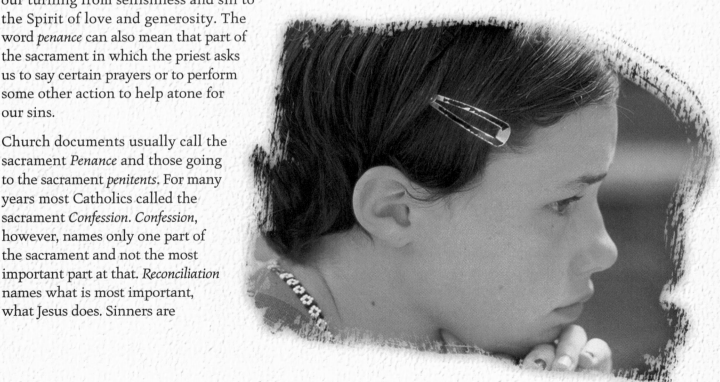

A Reconciling Church

Jesus called the Church to be a community of reconciliation and forgiveness. It is in his name and through his power that this forgiving and healing work continues in the Church. The ways in which the Church has answered this call have changed and developed over the centuries. We have seen how all our sins are forgiven when we are plunged into the death and resurrection of Jesus at Baptism. But what about sins committed after Baptism?

In the early Church these sins were forgiven by prayer, almsgiving, fasting, self-denial, and especially by the Eucharist. However, there were times when baptized Christians committed grave, public, and scandalous sins. Were these Christians still welcome at the Eucharist? Some process of conversion, repentance, and reconciliation had to take place first. The Church developed a ritual way to help the sinner repent, convert, and rejoin the community. This was called *canonical penance* because it was celebrated according to the *canons* (laws) of the Church. It was also modeled on the rite of Baptism, the first call to repentance.

The sinner came to the bishop, and they talked privately. Then, at Sunday Eucharist, the bishop prayed for the penitent and laid his hands on the sinner in a gesture of blessing and healing. A penance was given. The time of penance was long, often lasting several years or even the rest of the person's life.

Finally the day came for reconciliation. At Mass, after the readings and the homily, the penitent approached the bishop, they exchanged a kiss of peace, and the penitent was embraced once again as a member of the community. The penitent received the Eucharist and was reconciled with the community and with God.

This rite of penance was public. It involved the entire community, and it was a liturgical celebration. However, it was only for serious public sins and could be celebrated only once in a person's lifetime.

Later Developments

How did this public practice of the rite of Penance change? To help us understand this, we turn to fifth-century Ireland and Celtic monks. The Celts (the race of people who inhabited the island) had a different Church structure than that found in other countries. Their Christian life was organized around monasteries rather than cathedrals. Celtic monastic practices soon influenced the Church at large.

Celtic monks were accustomed to going to a holy person to ask for advice in overcoming their sins, just as today we might go to a doctor to ask for help and advice in overcoming a physical illness. Christians in fifth-century Ireland would seek out a holy person, tell their sins, and ask for healing. The "medicine" consisted of "healing by opposites." If one was a glutton, this could be healed by fasting. If one was lazy, this could be healed by rising early for prayer. This practice is called *Celtic penance.*

Celtic penance was very different from the canonical penance practiced in the rest of Europe. Canonical penance was only for grave public sins; Celtic penance was for all sins. Canonical penance was celebrated only once; Celtic penance was repeatable. Canonical penance involved the whole parish and was accompanied by liturgical rites; Celtic penance was a private affair.

Scripture UPDATE

The gospels clearly show that forgiveness of sins is central to the message of Jesus. Frequently in the gospels we see Jesus forgiving sins. He taught us to pray "Forgive us our trespasses, as we forgive those who trespass against us." And with his dying breath, he forgave even those who had nailed him to the cross.

During the seventh century Irish missionaries brought the practice of Celtic penance to Europe, and it eventually became the ordinary way that people celebrated the sacrament of Reconciliation. Confession was made to a priest who had the *power* to forgive sins in God's name. The penance the sinner was to perform was greatly reduced; for example, in place of "fasting for ten years," the penance might have been "say six Our Fathers."

The sacrament came to be seen in terms of a trial before a judge. The priest acted as judge. It was important to confess sins accurately, for a judge must have accurate knowledge on which to base his decision. The focus was on the judgment itself, the pronouncement of absolution. *Absolution* is pardon, or being set free, from sin. This understanding of the sacrament was common until the time of the Second Vatican Council.

In all of this, it is wonderful to see how the Spirit of God has continually guided the Church in its understanding of the sacrament of Reconciliation throughout history.

Read these passages from Luke's Gospel: 5:17–26; 7:36–50; 15:1–17. What is the attitude of Jesus toward the sinner? Is Jesus judge or healer?

The Communal Rite

The Second Vatican Council looked at this history of the various forms in which the Church has exercised the power to forgive sins. It revised the rites for Reconciliation to express more clearly what the sacrament really means and what it really does. These rites show that the sacrament is clearly a liturgical act. Like the Eucharist, Reconciliation celebrates the paschal mystery of Christ. Like the Eucharist, it consists of four parts: gathering, storytelling, the sacramental action, and commissioning.

There is no "one way" to celebrate this sacrament. Here is a general description of the *communal* celebration of the sacrament of Reconciliation.

Gathering The community gathers at the appointed time. There is a minister of hospitality at the door of the church to welcome us and to distribute any materials we may need to participate in the sacrament. The introductory rites usually include a hymn, a liturgical greeting, and a prayer by the priest to gather the assembly together.

Storytelling Once we are gathered, we tell the stories of God's love and mercy that are recorded in the Bible. The shape of this part of the rite is modeled on the Sunday Eucharist.

In hearing these stories of God's love, we come to see how much we are loved and to realize how little we have loved in return. The difference between these two loves— *how much* God has loved us and *how little* we have loved him—is called the "sense of sin." This is an important part of the sacramental process. It is the word of God that helps us to know our sinfulness.

Sin must be understood in relation to love. God has loved us so much, and we have so often failed to return that love. When we examine our lives in the light of the message of Jesus, we find that Jesus calls us to wholeness, to maturity. He came that we might have life and have it abundantly. For the Christian sin is not merely breaking the rules; it is the failure to grow. Sin is being today just as you were yesterday. Sin is the failure to respond to the love God has shown us in Christ Jesus.

After we have heard how much God loves us, we examine our lives to see how well we have loved God and our brothers and sisters in return. We examine our conscience in the light of the Scriptures. Together we express our sorrow in an Act of Contrition. Then we each confess our sins to a priest in private and hear the proclamation of God's forgiveness (absolution): "I *absolve* you." ("I pardon your sins.")

 In what ways do the Scriptures help us prepare for Reconciliation?

The Sacramental Action This prayer of absolution is the central prayer and sign of the sacrament of Reconciliation. As we have seen, the key prayer of each sacrament is usually a prayer blessing God in the form of a berakah. The sacrament of Reconciliation is an exception to this rule. The central prayer is not a berakah but a declaration: "I absolve you from your sins."

We have responded to the word of God by confessing our sins and receiving God's forgiveness. Now we celebrate this forgiveness, for it is God's response to *our* word. This part of the celebration might include a hymn, a proclamation of praise and thanksgiving for God's mercy, the Lord's Prayer, the kiss of peace, a song of thanksgiving, and a concluding prayer.

Commissioning The communal rite of Reconciliation concludes with prayers, blessings, and dismissal.

This declaration is expanded to mention the Father, the Son, and the Holy Spirit, for as we have seen, all liturgical prayer is prayer to the Trinity. The prayer of absolution mentions the principal effects of the sacrament: forgiveness, pardon, and peace.

The prayer of absolution that we hear each time we celebrate the sacrament is this:

> God, the Father of mercies,
> through the death and resurrection
>   of his Son
> has reconciled the world to himself
> and sent the Holy Spirit among us
> for the forgiveness of sins;
> through the ministry of the Church
> may God give you pardon and peace,
> and I absolve you from your sins
> in the name of the Father, and of the Son, †
> and of the Holy Spirit.

Our response is "Amen."

CATHOLIC TEACHINGS

About Reconciliation

Although confessing our venial sins and daily faults is encouraged, we are only *obliged* to confess individual sins to a priest when we are aware of having committed a *mortal sin* (a serious offense against God, done knowingly and freely, which cuts us off from the life of God and the Church). Catholics who are in the state of mortal sin and physically able must confess the sin to a priest in the sacrament of Reconciliation before they can receive Holy Communion.

Conversion of Heart

Catholics celebrate Reconciliation even when they have less serious sins to confess. Why? Because this sacrament is a great help to what Jesus wants for all his followers: conversion of heart.

In the life of the Church, the primary moment of conversion is the moment of Baptism. Yet conversion is not limited to that moment. It is the work of a lifetime. As followers of Christ we are called to a continual conversion of heart. One big "turning toward" God at Baptism is not enough for a full Christian life. We must continually turn toward God, as a growing plant continually turns toward its source of light, growth, and energy.

Conversion, our everyday turning away from evil and toward good, is not something we are expected to do on our own. Conversion is a grace of the Holy Spirit. Under the Spirit's guidance we are led to right thinking and good action. And with the help of the Spirit, we find the honesty to admit our failings and the courage to promise to do better. The sacrament of Reconciliation keeps us on track in our own individual work of conversion. It helps us to stop and reflect on how far we have come, and it helps us to resolve to continue the journey.

When the Fathers of the Church explained Baptism, they imagined an individual in the midst of a shipwreck. How to be saved in the midst of a raging sea? Grab a plank! This first plank is the sacrament of Baptism. When they taught about the sacrament of Reconciliation, they called it "the second plank" (*Catechism*, 1446). As Christians we need both to keep us afloat.

The Individual Rite

The individual rite of Reconciliation is another way the Church gives us to celebrate this sacrament. There are two important elements to this rite. As we learn about them, imagine yourself preparing to receive the sacrament. How would each of these elements apply to you?

The first element is human action: contrition, confession, and satisfaction (doing one's penance). The second element is God's action: the forgiveness of sins through the Church. Both our human actions and God's action are equally essential.

Contrition *Contrition* is sorrow for having sinned, detestation for the sin committed, and also a firm decision not to sin again. Before Reconciliation we should take time to make an examination of conscience and to ask ourselves if we really are sorry for our selfish actions and wrong choices.

Confession Confessing our sins to a priest is an essential part of this sacrament because the priest forgives sin in the name of Jesus Christ and the Church. Our sins are personal, but they are never private. We, the Church, are the body of Christ in the world. Sin affects the whole body of Christ. Just as in physical illness, when one part is in pain, the whole body suffers. The priest represents Christ and his body, so it is his task and joy to welcome sinners, as Jesus did, and to restore them to their rightful place in the body of Christ.

Sometimes people worry about what the priest thinks of them when they tell him their sins. They imagine that the priest sees them at their worst. Actually the very opposite is true. *Everybody* sins, but only *some* sinners are moved to do penance. When you tell your sins to the priest and express your desire to repent, the priest sees you at your best. The priest sees you, not in your sinning, but in your repentance.

Satisfaction *Satisfaction* is simply repairing, in some way, the harm our sins have done. Returning or paying for stolen goods, for example, is one obvious way of making satisfaction for the sin of stealing.

This kind of satisfaction is usually included in the *penance* given. A penance can be prayer, an offering, works of mercy, service to a neighbor, voluntary self-denial, sacrifices, and most of all a patient acceptance of the ordinary circumstances of our lives.

Reconciliation Now we turn to God's action in the sacrament of Reconciliation: the forgiveness of sins. Through this

forgiveness, as Pope John Paul II explained, we are reconciled with self, God, the entire Church, and "with all creation" (*Catechism*, 1469). Reconciliation is a sacrament of peace and comfort, a sacrament sealed in the conversational tones of a human voice: "I absolve you. . . . Go in the peace of Christ."

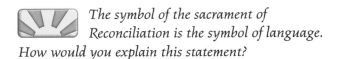

The symbol of the sacrament of Reconciliation is the symbol of language. How would you explain this statement?

The priest is strictly forbidden to use *in any way* anything he hears in the sacrament of Reconciliation. He can never, *never*, NEVER tell anyone what sin you confessed. If he does so, he himself commits a mortal sin. This obligation and promise is called the *seal of confession*. That is, the priest's lips are sealed, and he cannot reveal your sin or your identity.

things
to think about

What is helpful to you about talking to a priest? What would you talk to a priest about? As a teenager do you think you would ask advice in the sacrament of Reconciliation more often than you did in elementary school?

Do you prefer communal celebrations or celebrating the sacrament individually?

things
to share

Often the sacrament of Reconciliation is identified as a distinctively "Catholic" practice. How do other Christians seek forgiveness of their sins? How do they celebrate reconciliation? Talk to several of your friends who are not Catholics, and ask them how they experience the forgiveness of sins in their church community.

WORDS TO REMEMBER

Find and define the following:

Reconciliation _____
_____
_____

absolution _____
_____
_____

OnLine
WITH THE PARISH

When is the sacrament of Reconciliation celebrated in your parish? When are communal celebrations of the sacrament scheduled? When are opportunities available for celebrating the sacrament individually?

The communal celebration requires preparation and planning on the part of the parish liturgical team and also requires ministers: greeters, readers, musicians, and others. Is it possible for you to volunteer to serve in one of these ministries during the celebration?

What did Jesus teach us about the forgiveness of God?

1

Name the four parts of communal celebration of Reconciliation, and give a short explanation of each.

2

What are the human actions needed in Reconciliation? What is God's action?

3

When is a Catholic *obliged* to celebrate the sacrament of Reconciliation?

4

Of what value is Reconciliation in our continual conversion of heart?

5

Life in the Spirit

The Jesus Prayer is an ancient prayer that originated in the Eastern Church. It is still very well known and is used today, usually in this form: "Lord Jesus Christ, Son of the living God, have mercy on me, a sinner." This prayer reflects three Scripture passages: Philippians 2:6–11, Mark 10:46–52, and Luke 18:13. You might like to look these up and compare them with the Jesus Prayer.

Two familiar prayers in which we admit sin are the Hail Mary and the Our Father. Find a quiet time to pray one of these prayers or the Jesus Prayer this week. Ask for the grace of forgiving and being forgiven.

The Anointing
of the Sick

Even when I walk through a dark valley,
    I fear no harm for you are at my side....
You anoint my head with oil;
    my cup overflows.

Psalm 23:4–5

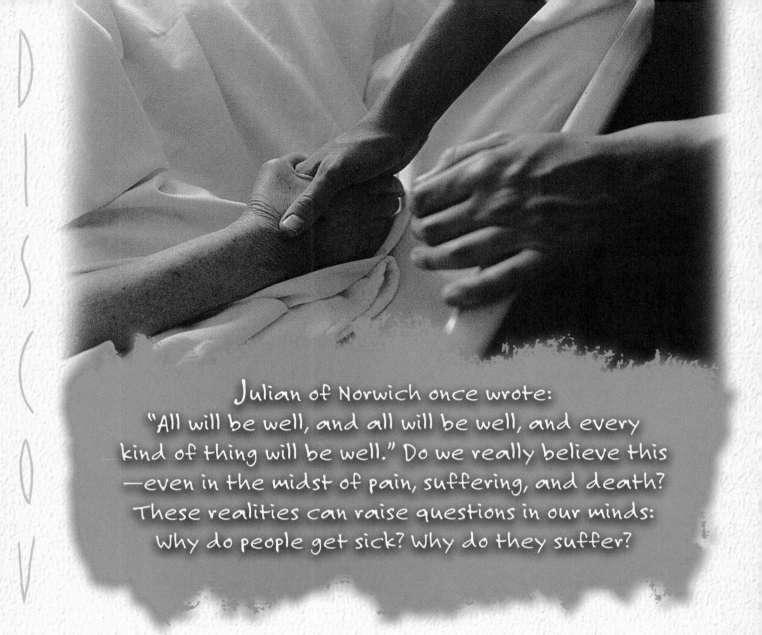

Julian of Norwich once wrote:
"All will be well, and all will be well, and every
kind of thing will be well." Do we really believe this
—even in the midst of pain, suffering, and death?
These realities can raise questions in our minds:
Why do people get sick? Why do they suffer?

The Mystery of Suffering

People have asked questions like these since the beginning of time!

There is no easy answer to the mystery of illness. It is one of those big questions whose answer is discovered bit by bit through our lived experience.

It is also a dangerous question because we can easily jump to overly simplified (and consequently, wrong) answers: "He got sick because he was bad." "She is ill because God wants her to suffer." It is very dangerous to think in this way, for such thinking leads to false conclusions about suffering and false conclusions about God.

We know that God created us out of love, and that creation is holy and good. Suffering and illness do not exist because God wants them to exist. But if they do not come from him, where do they come from?

Sometimes, but not always, they come from our own ignorance and poor decisions. We have the responsiblity to care for our bodies, to be attentive to proper nourishment, exercise, rest, and relaxation. Pain is often a message from the body telling us that something is wrong, that something needs to be corrected or cared for.

Human illness can urge us to learn more about the functions of the body through the study of chemistry, biology, physiology, and other sciences. In so doing, perhaps we can help others someday. Even more important, illness is a call to learn more about our inner selves, about life and its meaning.

We know that one of the hardest things about being sick is the sudden end to our ordinary activities at school, with friends, in sports, and so on. Much of the way we think about ourselves is tied up with what we can do. When our health is taken away, we find that we cannot do very much! Then we begin to wonder who we really are.

But faith gives us a new way of seeing illness. In God's eyes we are more than what we do, more than our accomplishments. The world often judges people by how much money they make, by how many things they have. Illness can remind us that God loves us for who we are, not for what we have or what we do.

Jesus and Healing

We know about God's love and concern for the sick because we can see it made visible in Jesus. On almost every page of the gospels, we see Jesus bringing health and wholeness to those who are ill and suffering.

Look, for example, at the first chapter of Mark's Gospel. After Jesus called the first disciples, he cured a man with an unclean spirit; then he cured Peter's mother-in-law, who was in bed with a fever. Mark continues: "When it was evening, after sunset, they brought to him all who were ill or possessed by demons. The whole town was gathered at the door. He cured many who were sick with various diseases, and he drove out many demons" (1:32–34). Mark tells us that Jesus' reputation as a healer spread so far and wide that "it was impossible for Jesus to enter a town openly. He remained outside in deserted places, and people kept coming to him from everywhere" (Mark 1:45).

All this takes place in just the first chapter of Mark's Gospel! Jesus has hardly begun his ministry, but already he is known as someone who heals the sick and cares for them.

Jesus himself is a visible sign of God's desire for our health and wholeness. Jesus "spoke to them of the kingdom of God, and he healed those who needed to be cured" (Luke 9:11). When we see Jesus in this way as a sign of God's healing, we are well on our way to understanding the Church as a sign of healing. The Church exercises this ministry in many ways and celebrates it in the sacrament of the Anointing of the Sick.

Jesus Heals a Blind Man,
Duccio di Buoninsegna,
thirteenth century

129

Healing in the Early Church

Jesus' desire to heal the sick did not stop when he ascended into heaven. He had told his disciples to continue this work: "So.... they anointed with oil many who were sick and cured them" (Mark 6:12–13).

In the Letter of James, we read of the way in which one early Christian community continued this healing work of Jesus. "Is anyone among you suffering? He should pray. Is anyone in good spirits? He should sing praise. Is anyone among you sick? He should summon the presbyters of the church, and they should pray over him and anoint [him] with oil in the name of the Lord, and the prayer of faith will save the sick person, and the Lord will raise him up. If he has committed any sins, he will be forgiven" (James 5:13–15).

James tells us that prayer is necessary in every situation in our lives: when we are well, when we are sick, and at every moment in between. Look at the passage from the Letter of James again. Prayer is mentioned in every verse. It is in this context of prayer that James tells us of his community's practice of praying for the sick. The sick person calls for the priests. When they arrive, they pray. The phrase "pray over" the sick person suggests a laying on of hands, the ancient sign of blessing. They anoint the sick person with oil.

The community of that time would have been familiar with the use of oil as a common medicine. People rubbed oil on their bodies as an ointment to heal and strengthen and preserve. In the story of the Good Samaritan, we read that when the Samaritan found the man who had fallen prey to robbers, he bandaged the man's wounds and poured oil on them (Luke 10:34).

Healing and Anointing

The rites that the Church uses to continue the healing ministry of Jesus have changed and developed through the centuries, just as the "rites" medical doctors use to cure and heal have changed. Going to the doctor in times past was a different experience from a visit to the doctor today.

When Saint Francis of Assisi suffered from severe pains in his eyes, the doctor heated metal axheads in a fire and, when they were red-hot, pressed them to Francis's temples so that the burning irons would draw the pain out of his eyes. When we consider the common medical practices of those times, we see why one would put off going to the doctor as long as possible! If the disease didn't kill you, the doctor probably would.

In the same time period, when priests and teachers explained the meaning of the rites of anointing, they drew a parallel between physical healing by medical doctors and spiritual healing administered by the Church. Many good things can be learned from this analogy. But one bad effect it had was that the Church's anointing was put off as long as possible, just as going to the doctor was put off until the sick person was at death's door. The sacramental anointing (*unction* in Latin) came to be called *Extreme Unction*, the last anointing. The sacrament for the *sick* became a sacrament only for the *dying*. The priest's final absolution of our sins and this anointing at the time of death came to be called the *last rites*.

OI stands for Oleum Infirmorum (*Latin for* Oil of the Sick).

The focus of the sacrament then changed from physical healing to spiritual healing, to the forgiveness of sins. The public, liturgical rite of the early Church became a private ceremony. Often only the priest and the dying person were present. Extreme Unction had become more private than public, more fearful than joyful, and more dreaded than celebrated. For many Catholics, when the priest arrived with the holy oil for the last rites, it was a sure sign of death.

Catholics experienced Extreme Unction in this way from the Middle Ages until the Second Vatican Council in this century. Following the liturgical reforms of this Council, Extreme Unction became once again the sacrament of the Anointing of the Sick as we know it today.

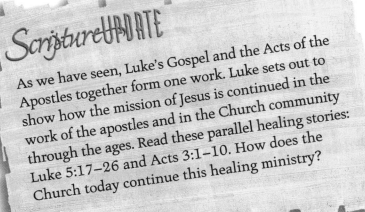

*Scripture*UPDATE

As we have seen, Luke's Gospel and the Acts of the Apostles together form one work. Luke sets out to show how the mission of Jesus is continued in the work of the apostles and in the Church community through the ages. Read these parallel healing stories: Luke 5:17–26 and Acts 3:1–10. How does the Church today continue this healing ministry?

 Take a moment to think of those "among you" who are sick. Pray for them now.

Not Just for the Dying

To remove the atmosphere of hesitation and fear that surrounded Extreme Unction, the Second Vatican Council made three important changes.

First, it was important to teach that this sacrament is not just intended for the dying, that it is primarily a sacrament of healing for all Christians who are seriously ill. It can be received more than once—each time, in fact, that a Christian becomes seriously ill, and again if the illness worsens. So the Council suggested that we call this sacrament not Extreme Unction but the sacrament of the *Anointing of the Sick.*

Second, this sacrament of healing was restored to its liturgical (public) setting. No longer was it to be considered a private action between the priest and the sick person. The community's role of prayerful support was restored, and the celebration of the Anointing of the Sick within the Eucharist was encouraged.

Third, the focus of the sacrament was directed once again toward *healing.* In anointing the hands of the sick, the priest leads the community in prayer:

> May the Lord who frees you from sin
> save you and raise you up.

We pray that our sick brothers and sisters will be raised up to share in the life of the resurrected Jesus—both physically and spiritually.

Celebration of Anointing

The celebration of the sacrament may take various forms: It may take place at a Sunday or weekday Mass in a parish church, in the home of the sick person, in the hospital, or in an emergency situation. Here is a general description of the way the sacrament is celebrated at the Sunday liturgy.

Gathering The parish Eucharist begins as usual. Sometimes the sick, along with the whole congregation, are blessed with baptismal water. In Baptism we died with Christ; the suffering that these sick persons are now experiencing is part of that dying.

Storytelling We then read from the Sacred Scriptures and hear how Christ has conquered suffering and death by his own death and resurrection. Usually the readings assigned for the Sunday are appropriate because nearly every page of Scripture speaks of God's desire for our health and healing.

The homily relates the readings to the Christian meaning of suffering. Those who are ill or suffering can freely and lovingly choose to unite their sufferings with the sufferings of Christ. Following the homily we join in a litany of intercession for the sick, for the parish, and for the needs of the world.

Imposition of Hands Those to be anointed are invited to come forward. With silent and intense prayer to the Holy Spirit, the priest lays his hands on the head of each person. This is one of the key symbolic actions of the sacrament. The gesture indicates that this particular person is the object of the Church's prayer. It is a sign of blessing. Most important, it was Jesus' own gesture of healing: "At sunset, all who had people sick with various diseases brought them to him. He laid his hands on each of them and cured them" (Luke 4:40).

Invocation The priest blesses God for the gift of oil. Olive oil reminds us of the suffering of Jesus in the Garden of Olives (Luke 22:39–46). The oil is blessed by the bishop of the diocese on Holy Thursday. It is this blessing that makes the oil sacramental. Sometimes the priest blesses the oil at the time of anointing. He prays:

God of all consolation,
you chose and sent your Son to heal the world.
Graciously listen to our prayer of faith:
send the power of your Holy Spirit, the Consoler,
into this precious oil, this soothing ointment,
this rich gift, this fruit of the earth.

Bless this oil † and sanctify it for our use.

Make this oil a remedy for all who are anointed
    with it;
heal them in body, in soul, and in spirit,
and deliver them from every affliction.
We ask this through our Lord Jesus Christ, your
    Son,
who lives and reigns with you and the Holy Spirit,
one God, for ever and ever.
Amen.

Anointing with Oil Next we see the essential rite of the sacrament. The priest anoints each sick person with the oil. He makes the sign of the cross first on the person's forehead and then on the palm of each hand. He prays that God in his love and mercy will "raise" the sick person to health. We all respond, "Amen."

Look again at the blessing of the oil of the sick. What does the prayer say about God? About oil? What does it ask for the sick?

CATHOLIC TEACHINGS

About Viaticum

In addition to the sacrament of the Anointing of the Sick, the Church provides another great gift to those who are close to death: the Eucharist. Holy Communion given to the dying is called *Viaticum*, a word from Latin that literally means "with you on the way." Communion has a special significance when received at the close of life. "It is the seed of eternal life and the power of the resurrection" (*Catechism*, 1524).

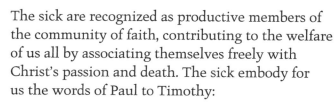

An Exchange of Signs

In the liturgy signs are given and signs are received. The care and concern of the Christian community is a sign to the sick person of the Lord's own great concern for the bodily and spiritual welfare of the sick. We who are the body of Christ must continue to proclaim the kingdom of wholeness and salvation in word and deed.

The celebration of the sacrament of the Anointing of the Sick is a ritual moment that makes visible and present to the sick and to the whole community who we are as Church: a community of healing and support. That is why the whole parish community is invited to come together in prayerful support of those among us who are in special need.

The sick, in return, offer a sign to the community: In this sacrament they give witness to their promises at Baptism to die with Christ and be buried with him. They tell the community that they are prepared to offer their suffering, in union with Christ's, for the good of the whole Church and the salvation of the world.

This exchange of signs between the sick and the healthy members of the community is at the heart of the sacrament. The sick are assured in the ritual that their suffering is not useless, that it is a sharing in the saving work of Jesus. Their sins are forgiven. At the same time the Church asks the Lord to lighten their suffering, to give them peace and courage, and to save them.

The sick are recognized as productive members of the community of faith, contributing to the welfare of us all by associating themselves freely with Christ's passion and death. The sick embody for us the words of Paul to Timothy:

> If we have died with him
> we shall also live with him. . . .
> 2 Timothy 2:11

For All Ages

Who can receive anointing? How sick does one have to be in order to be anointed? The Church tells us that the sacrament is for those whose health is seriously impaired by sickness or old age. One does *not* have to be in danger of death. The sacrament is most fruitful when the person being anointed is well enough to participate fully in it.

A person can be anointed before surgery when a serious illness or disability is the reason for the operation. In this case it is preferable to celebrate the sacrament even before the person goes to the hospital.

134

There are times when old age and the fear and loneliness that can sometimes come with it need to be brought to the healing presence of Christ in this sacrament. At the same time it is important to avoid identifying illness with certain age groups. Today we do not automatically equate high numerical age with fragile health, weakness, or inactivity.

The sacrament is for all ages and all types of illness. Sick children who have sufficient use of reason to be strengthened by the sacrament can be anointed. Persons with the disease of alcoholism or suffering from other addictions can be anointed, as can those who suffer from various mental disorders.

But the big question is, "Does it work?" Does the sick person experience healing? The answer is yes. The sacrament is the prayer of the Church, the body of Christ. Christ himself has assured us that whatever we ask the Father in his name will be granted.

People who have been anointed are eager to tell of the healing that they experienced. And often the stories they tell are of wonderful, unexplainable healing. Sometimes, for others, the stories are less spectacular. But some form of healing does take place. It is not always physical healing; sometimes it is a healing of the spirit. The sacrament is never a substitute for the work of doctors and nurses, drugs and hospitals. God's healing power also works through the hands and intelligence of medical professionals.

In the sacrament we pray that the sick be healed in body, in soul, and in spirit. God knows more than we do what healing the sick person might need most: that a wound be healed, that a fear turn to confidence, that loneliness disappear, that bafflement in the face of all the whys—Why me? Why suffering? Why now?—may turn into understanding. Ultimately we pray that the sacrament of the Anointing of the Sick will give us a better understanding of the mystery of a loving God who raised his crucified Son, bearing his victorious wounds, to be with the Father in glory.

 Describe what you think is meant by spiritual healing.

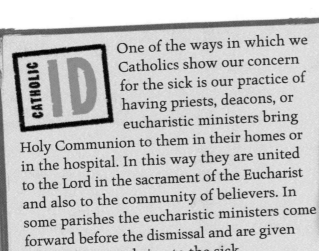

One of the ways in which we Catholics show our concern for the sick is our practice of having priests, deacons, or eucharistic ministers bring Holy Communion to them in their homes or in the hospital. In this way they are united to the Lord in the sacrament of the Eucharist and also to the community of believers. In some parishes the eucharistic ministers come forward before the dismissal and are given the Eucharist to bring to the sick.

What are some other ways in which we show our concern for the sick?

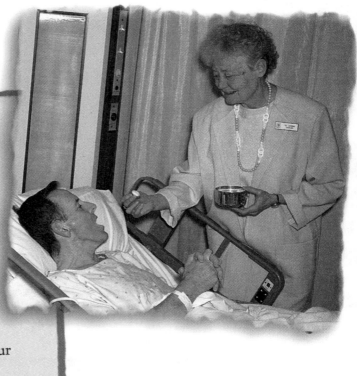

135

things
to think about

Have you ever been present at the sacrament of the Anointing of the Sick? Describe the experience.

Sometimes we tend to ignore or forget about people we know who are ill. How would being prayerfully present at this sacrament help those who are not receiving it?

WORDS TO REMEMBER

Find and define the following:

Anointing of the Sick _____
_____
_____

Viaticum _____
_____
_____

things
to share

Talk to someone who has received the sacrament of the Anointing of the Sick. Ask what the experience was like. Did he or she experience healing? In what way?

OnLine
WITH THE PARISH

When is the sacrament of the Anointing of the Sick scheduled in your parish? Often at these times volunteers are needed to help care for the sick and to exercise various liturgical ministries during the celebration. Sometimes a meal is served afterward. Could you offer your help on these occasions?

In what other ways does your parish reach out to the sick? When can you take time to visit and pray with the homebound?

1. How do we know about God's love and concern for the sick? Give two examples from the gospels.

2. List three ways in which the sacrament of the Anointing of the Sick is different from Extreme Unction.

3. What different forms of celebration may the sacrament of the Anointing of the Sick take?

4. Who can receive this sacrament? How sick does a person have to be to receive it?

5. How does a communal celebration of the sacrament of the Anointing of the Sick benefit the whole parish?

Life in the Spirit

The prayer below was written by Saint Richard of Chichester, an English bishop who cared for the poor and the needy. Use it as a prayer of thanksgiving and as a prayer of discipleship, asking for the grace to follow Jesus each day, in sickness and in health!

Thanks be to you, Lord Jesus Christ,
for all the benefits and blessings which you have given to me....
O most merciful friend, brother, and redeemer,
may I know you more clearly,
love you more dearly,
and follow you more nearly.

CHAPTER 12

The Sacrament of Holy Orders

How beautiful upon the mountains
are the feet of him who brings glad tidings,
Announcing peace, bearing good news.

Isaiah 52:7

The priesthood is essential to the life of the Church. Why do you think this is so?

The Call to Holy Orders

Each of us was called at Baptism to share in the priesthood of Christ. We share in his priesthood by living out our baptismal promises and by continuing Christ's work on earth. The sacraments of Baptism and Confirmation consecrate each Christian for the common priesthood of the faithful. We are not ordained ministers, but we are called to share the good news of Christ and to carry on his mission in the world.

Some, however, are called to share in Christ's priesthood in a unique way as his ordained ministers. In the sacrament of Holy Orders, men are consecrated for a special life of sacramental ministry to the body of Christ, the Church. What makes the ordained ministry different?

Holy Orders is the sacrament through which the mission and authority Christ gave his apostles continues in the Church. "The Church confers the sacrament of Holy Orders only on baptized men" (*Catechism*, 1598). The sacrament includes three ranks, or orders:

- the episcopate (bishops)
- the presbyterate (priests)
- the diaconate (deacons).

In this chapter we will look at each of these orders and examine the ways in which each is celebrated in the liturgy of the Church. In general, however, we can say that in Holy Orders a man shares in the priesthood in three essential ways: ministry, divine worship, and authority.

Ministry   Before Christ ascended into heaven, he gave his apostles this mandate:

> Go, therefore, and make disciples of all nations, baptizing them in the name of the Father, and of the Son, and of the holy Spirit, teaching them to observe all that I have commanded you. And behold, I am with you always, until the end of the age.
> Matthew 28:19–20

Those ordained to ministry today have the same mandate: to bring the gospel to all people and to baptize them in the name of the Trinity.

All ministry is service, and Jesus made it quite clear that his ministers were to be the servants of the Church. At the Last Supper he washed the feet of his apostles, symbolically demonstrating their call to service. He told them that he "did not come to be served but to serve" (Mark 10:45).

We read in the Acts of the Apostles that after Jesus Christ ascended to his Father and after the coming of the Holy Spirit, the apostles led the early Church in two ways:

- They traveled through the known world preaching the good news of salvation through Jesus Christ.
- They taught and passed on to the early followers of Jesus their lived memories of his words and actions, especially of his death and resurrection.

"With great power the apostles bore witness to the resurrection of the Lord Jesus" (Acts 4:33).

Divine Worship   At the Last Supper Jesus gave the Church his own Body and Blood in the Eucharist and told his apostles to "do this in memory of me" (Luke 22:19). The ordained ministers of the Church celebrate the Eucharist and the other sacraments with the people of God.

Priests share in Christ's priesthood to the highest degree in the Eucharist. In this divine worship they act in the person of Christ himself. They proclaim and offer to the Father Christ's paschal mystery, for "in the sacrifice of the Mass they make present again and apply, until the coming of the Lord, the unique sacrifice of the New Testament" — Christ himself (*Catechism*, 1566).

Clearly it is in the holy Eucharist that the whole ministry of the priest draws its strength.

Authority   Ordained ministers share in the authority of Jesus Christ. In the gospel we see Jesus sending his disciples out to teach, to baptize, to heal, and to forgive with this authority.

After the resurrection the Church grew very rapidly as more and more people joined the Christian community. The apostles chose others to help them in their work of teaching and leading the Church in worship and service. The apostles laid their hands on them and prayed that the Holy Spirit would strengthen them. In time these successors of the apostles, as we will see, were called bishops. Bishops in turn ordained priests to help them in the work of ministry. The authority of bishops and priests comes, not from themselves, but from Jesus Christ.

"No one can give himself the mandate and the mission to proclaim the Gospel. The one sent by the Lord does not speak and act on his own authority, but by virtue of Christ's authority" (*Catechism*, 875).

Holy Orders is the sacrament through which the mission given by Christ to the apostles continues in the Church today. The sacrament confers an indelible mark. As in the sacraments of Baptism and Confirmation, this unique sharing in the priesthood of Christ is given only once; it cannot be repeated. One who is ordained is ordained forever.

A new bishop receives the ring, symbol of fidelity.

The Apostolic Call

Jesus knew that he could not do his work for the kingdom alone. He needed helpers to carry out his mission of preaching God's love, healing the sick, and reconciling sinners. In the Gospel of Luke, we read that before choosing his apostles, Jesus spent the whole night in prayer: "In those days he departed to the mountain to pray, and he spent the night in prayer to God. When day came, he called his disciples to himself, and from them he chose Twelve, whom he also named apostles" (Luke 6:12–13).

These apostles, as we know from the accounts given in the Acts of the Apostles, did carry out the work of Jesus. They were the first missionaries. They founded and guided local churches. When the need arose, they met together to consider the best decision to make for the life and growth of the Church.

In time the apostles ordained others to follow in their footsteps. From one generation to the next, new apostolic leaders have been called and ordained to service in the Church. Our bishops today are successors to the apostles, for they share to the fullest extent in the grace of Holy Orders. Bishops teach, govern, and sanctify with the authority of Christ. In his local church the bishop is the chief teacher, the chief governor, and the chief priest. The bishop is the leader of the local church, whether that local church is the church of New York, the church of Los Angeles, the church of Tulsa, the church of Paris, the church of Bangkok, or the church of Rio de Janeiro.

But the responsibilities of a bishop are not confined to his own local church. The bishop is also responsible, under the leadership of the bishop of Rome, the pope, and together with all the other bishops, for the teaching, governance, and sanctification of the entire Church throughout the world. Bishops often meet together to discuss current issues facing the Church and the world. Bishops also meet regularly with the pope on an individual basis. In this way the pope and each bishop can confer about the particular needs of a local church. This visit to the pope is called the *ad limina* visit. This term literally means "to the doorstep" in Latin. The bishop is invited to the pope's doorstep because the life and welfare of each local church is vital to the whole body of Christ.

The Ordination of a Bishop

A bishop is ordained by other bishops. Only bishops can lay hands in ordination of a newly chosen bishop. The ordination takes place during the Eucharist, after the reading of the gospel. First a mandate, or letter, from the Holy Father is read, confirming the ordination of the new bishop.

Receiving the miter

Then the people of the local church are asked to give their consent to the ordination. The congregation usually responds with enthusiastic applause. A homily is given by the principal ordaining bishop. He then asks the newly chosen bishop, or bishop-elect, a series of questions. By his answers the bishop-elect declares his readiness to serve his people.

During the Litany of the Saints, the bishop-elect prostrates himself; that is, he lies facedown on the floor as he asks the help of the Church in heaven. Prostration is an ancient symbol of humble and sincere prayer.

The principal ordaining bishop prays that the Lord will anoint his servant, the bishop-elect, "with the fullness of priestly grace." This bishop, in complete silence, lays his hands on the head of the bishop-elect. The other bishops present then do the same. This ritual action, along with the prayer of consecration, is the visible sign of the ordination of a bishop.

While the Book of the Gospels is held above the new bishop's head, the principal ordaining bishop offers the prayer of consecration. The new bishop's head is anointed with oil, the same oil used in the sacraments of Baptism and Confirmation. The Book of the Gospels, which symbolizes the bishop's role as teacher and preacher of the word of God, is then given to the new bishop.

He is also given a ring as a symbol of fidelity to the Church. He receives the miter and, with these words, the crosier, or pastoral staff:

Take this staff as a sign of your pastoral office:
keep watch over the whole flock
in which the Holy Spirit has appointed you
to shepherd the Church of God.

The new bishop is then invited to take his seat in the chair of the bishop, the *cathedra*, and all the bishops exchange the sign of peace.

At the end of the Eucharist, the new bishop himself may give the solemn blessing. He may say:

Lord God,
now that you have raised me to the order of bishops,
may I please you in the performance of my office.
Unite the hearts of people and bishop,
so that the shepherd may not be without the support of his flock,
or the flock without the loving concern of its shepherd.

All respond, "Amen."

The new bishop then blesses the people.

Who is the bishop of your diocese? What are some ways you can support your bishop?

The Priesthood of Christ

There are many bishops and many priests, but there is only one priesthood, the priesthood of Christ. Saint Paul explained that Jesus Christ is the one priest, the one mediator between God and the human race:

> For there is one God.
> There is also one mediator between God
>   and the human race,
> Christ Jesus, himself human,
> who gave himself as ransom for all.
> 1 Timothy 2:5–6

The unique sacrifice of Jesus Christ on the cross is made present in the Eucharist. In the same way the one priesthood of Christ is made present in the priesthood of his ministers: our bishops, priests (presbyters), and deacons. This priesthood is the means that Christ chose to build up and lead the Church. Through the ordained ministry of bishops and priests, the presence of Christ as head of the Church is made visible. Through the sacrament of Holy Orders, bishops and priests are ordained to bring this unique presence of Christ to us.

Priests and bishops act not only in the name of Christ but also in the name of the whole Church, especially at the Eucharist, in which they present the entire body of Christ to God. It is because they represent Christ that they also represent the body of Christ, the Church. To share in the priesthood of Christ means to share in the work of Christ as mediator between God and the human race. It is the work of the priest, in all that he does, to serve the people of God.

In this work the priest is a coworker with the bishop. In Holy Orders priests are united with the bishop in the priesthood of Christ. The priest is consecrated and ordained to preach the gospel, to celebrate the sacraments, and to guide the members of the body of Christ. He does this under the authority of his bishop.

When he is ordained, the new priest makes a promise of obedience to the bishop of the local church in which he will serve. At the end of the ordination rite, the bishop and the new priest exchange the sign of peace. Both actions are signs that the priest and his bishop are united in working for the kingdom of God. The bishop needs priests to help him and considers the priests of his diocese his "co-workers, his sons, his brothers and his friends" (*Catechism*, 1567).

What do you think is the main work of a priest? Why is it essential to the Church?

The Ordination of a Priest

The ordination of a priest is very much like the ordination of a bishop. The essential rite of the sacrament—the laying on of hands and the prayer of consecration—is the same except that after the bishop lays hands on the candidate, the other priests present also lay their hands on him. This is a sign of their unity, of working together for the kingdom.

The rite of the ordination of a priest takes place during the Eucharist, after the reading of the gospel. The candidate is called forward and presented to the bishop. After the bishop is assured that the candidate is prepared for the priesthood, the bishop says:

We rely on the help of the Lord God and our Savior Jesus Christ, and we choose this man, our brother, for priesthood in the presbyteral order.

The consent of the people is then given, usually by joyful applause.

The bishop gives a homily explaining that the candidate "is to serve Christ the Teacher, Priest, and Shepherd in his ministry which is to make his own body, the Church, grow into the people of God, a holy temple." The bishop then asks the candidate, in a series of questions, if he is willing to carry out the duties of a priest. The candidate answers, "I am, with the help of God."

The candidate promises obedience to the bishop of the local church under whom he will serve. After the bishop leads a prayer for the candidate, the candidate prostrates himself during the Litany of the Saints. The bishop asks God the Father to pour out upon the candidate the blessing of the Holy Spirit and the grace and power of the priesthood.

Then, in silence, the bishop lays his hands on the candidate's head. Still in silence, all the priests who are present also lay their hands upon the candidate. The bishop, extending his hands over the candidate, offers the prayer of consecration. These two actions—the laying on of hands followed by the prayer of consecration—are the essential signs of ordination.

Scripture UPDATE

In Luke's Gospel we read that Jesus sent out the Twelve to minister to the people. Take the time to read Luke 9:1–6 to discover what the apostles were commissioned to do and what power and authority they were given.

The new priest is invested with the stole and chasuble as symbols of the priesthood. Next the bishop anoints the palms of the new priest's hands with chrism, the same oil used in Baptism and Confirmation. After the gifts of bread and wine are presented, the bishop gives the paten and chalice to the new priest with these words:

> Accept from the holy people of God the
>   gifts to be offered to him.
> Know what you are doing, and imitate
>   the mystery you celebrate:
> model your life on the mystery of the
>   Lord's cross.

Then the bishop and the newly ordained exchange a sign of peace, and the celebration of the Eucharist continues.

Describe what is happening in each picture.

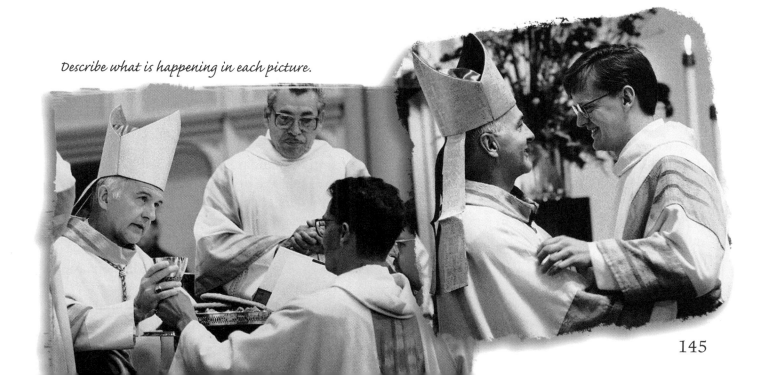

Ordained for Service

The word *deacon* comes from a Greek word meaning "to serve." The first deacons were called to serve by providing food for the poor of the early Church. We read in the Acts of the Apostles that the Church in Jerusalem was growing so quickly that the daily distribution of food was not being taken care of properly. Some groups were complaining of neglect. So the apostles met with the community and said, "'It is not right for us to neglect the word of God to serve at table. Brothers, select from among you seven reputable men, filled with the Spirit and wisdom, whom we shall appoint to this task…' The proposal was acceptable to the whole community" (Acts 6:2–5).

The first deacon chosen was Stephen, "a man filled with faith and the holy Spirit" (Acts 6:5), who is now honored as the patron saint of all deacons. To carry out his task, Stephen was given wonderful gifts from God. He was "filled with grace and power" (Acts 6:8), and no one could deny "the wisdom and the spirit with which he spoke" (Acts 6:10). When Stephen was brought before the religious judges to defend himself against false charges, the officials "saw that his face was like the face of an angel" (Acts 6:15). This means that they recognized Stephen to be "like an angel" — a true messenger from God.

Like Stephen, deacons today carry God's message to us and share in the mission of Christ through the grace of Holy Orders. They are marked with an indelible spiritual character that conforms them to Christ, "who made himself the 'deacon' or servant of all" (*Catechism*, 1570). Deacons today may perform their service to the Church in many ways: in assisting the bishops and priests in the liturgy, above all in the Eucharist; in the distribution of communion; in assisting at and blessing marriages; in the proclaiming of the gospel and in preaching; in presiding over funerals; and in works of service and charity. In all these tasks the deacon is guided first of all by the bishop of the local church and then by the pastor of the parish in which he serves.

The Ordination of a Deacon

The ordination of a deacon is similar to that of a bishop or priest except that at a deacon's ordination only the bishop lays hands on the candidate. This symbolizes the deacon's special attachment to the bishop in the tasks of his service.

The ordination of a deacon, like that of a bishop and a priest, takes place at the celebration of the Eucharist. After the reading of the gospel, the candidate is called forward, the bishop is assured of his worthiness, and the people assent to ordination by enthusiastic applause. In his homily the bishop explains the role of a deacon: "He will draw new strength from the gift of the Holy Spirit. He will help the bishop and his body of priests as a minister of the word, of the altar, and of charity. He will make himself a servant to all."

If an unmarried deacon intends to remain celibate, or if he intends to be ordained to the priesthood at a future time, he now makes a promise of lifelong celibacy. *Celibacy* means remaining unmarried for the sake of the kingdom of God.

Next the candidate is questioned by the bishop, who asks if the deacon-elect is willing to be ordained for ministry and if he is resolved to carry out its responsibilities. The candidate answers, "I am, with the help of God."

After the Litany of the Saints, the bishop lays his hands, in silence, on the candidate's head. Then, with his hands extended over the candidate, the bishop prays the prayer of consecration.

The deacon is given a deacon's stole and the special deacon's vestment called the dalmatic. He wears the stole, not around his neck as a priest does, but diagonally across his chest. Now vested as a deacon, the newly ordained minister kneels before the bishop and receives from him the Book of the Gospels. The bishop instructs the new deacon:

Receive the Gospel of Christ,
whose herald you now are.
Believe what you read,
teach what you believe,
and practice what you teach.

The whole Church rejoices in the ordination of a new servant, a new herald, a new messenger, a new Stephen for our times.

 In what ways is a deacon to be a servant and a herald?

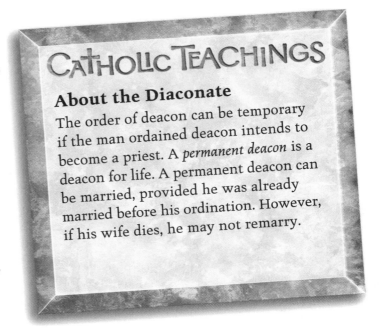

CATHOLIC TEACHINGS

About the Diaconate

The order of deacon can be temporary if the man ordained deacon intends to become a priest. A *permanent deacon* is a deacon for life. A permanent deacon can be married, provided he was already married before his ordination. However, if his wife dies, he may not remarry.

Here is a brief summary of Holy Orders to help you recall the main ideas of this chapter.

Three Ranks	Who Ordains?	Essential Signs	Ministry
bishop (episcopate)	Only a bishop can ordain another bishop, a priest, or a deacon.	the laying on of hands and the prayer of consecration	successor to the apostles leader of his local church chief teacher, governor, and priest for his diocese in union with the pope and the other bishops, responsible for the teaching, governance, and sanctification of the entire Church
priest (presbyterate)	A priest is ordained by a bishop, usually the bishop of his diocese.	same as above	coworker with the bishop in preaching the gospel, celebrating the sacraments, and guiding the members of the body of Christ
deacon (diaconate)	A deacon is ordained by the bishop of his diocese.	same as above	assists the bishops and priests in works of service and charity and, in the liturgy, proclaiming the gospel and preaching

things to think about

What do you think Jesus meant when he said that he came "not to be served but to serve"? How do ordained ministers try to serve as Christ served?

Why would you think a bishop, priest, or deacon must be a person of prayer?

things to share

The priesthood is not something a person decides to do on his own. No one has the *right* to receive Holy Orders. He must submit his desire to the authority of the Church because only the Church has the right to call a person to receive orders.

How, then, does the vocation of the priest differ from that of a doctor, for example, or from that of married people?

WORDS TO REMEMBER

Find and define the following:

Holy Orders _____
_____
_____

deacon _____
_____
_____

OnLine WITH THE PARISH

Many parishes have a yearly thank-you celebration for all the people who volunteer to help the parish in every area of service. If your parish sponsors such an event, volunteer to help in some way.

Maybe your group would like to sponsor "thank-you day" for your parish priests and deacons. You might ask one of the parish groups to help you organize it as an appreciation for those ordained to serve us in Christ day after day.

What are the three degrees of the sacrament of Holy Orders?

1

In what three special ways does an ordained man share in the priesthood of Christ?

2

What is the relationship between today's bishops and the first apostles?

3

What is the relationship between the bishop and the priests in his diocese?

4

What is the work of a deacon in the Church?

5

Life in the Spirit

Pope John XXIII had a favorite saying: "Let us leave the past to God's mercy, the present to his love, and the future to his providence." Use these prayers to help you follow God's will for you in the present and prepare for God's plan for your future:

Show me the path I should walk, for to you I entrust my life.
Psalm 143:8

The LORD will guard you from all evil,
will always guard your life.
The LORD will guard your coming and going
both now and forever.
Psalm 121:7–8

CHAPTER 13

The Sacrament of Matrimony

God is love,
and whoever remains
in love remains in God.

1 John 4:16

A wise priest counsels a young couple: "Remember, a wedding lasts an hour; a marriage lasts a lifetime." What do you think this means?

The Sacrament of Matrimony

Weddings are beautiful ceremonies. Whether large or small, weddings are intended to be celebrations of love; and as many people say, love makes the world go round. But is this simple understanding of love enough to make a marriage last? Is there more to marriage than the feeling of romance we see so often in movies, on television, and in the books and magazines we read? What are we to think as Catholics and members of the Church, the body of Christ? Let's take a long look at the wonder and mystery of marriage.

Obviously the civil authorities think there is more to marriage than movies or television portray. Take the United States, for example. Each year thousands of men and women obtain a civil license from the state in which they want to be married, and each state has special requirements that must be fulfilled if a marriage is to be considered legal. These may include an age requirement or even the taking of a blood test as a check to keep society free from communicable diseases. Then every couple must pay for a marriage license—which may be easier to get than a driver's license!

Why is the state so interested in marriage? Because marriage is so important for society. In fact society is built on marriage and the family. We as a society must know when two people are promising to share responsibility for rearing children, owning property, and paying taxes. Without marriage and family life, society would fall apart in ruins. The state wants to make sure that all is well for those who want to be married. Healthy marriages mean a healthy society everywhere in the world.

But after thinking about romance and society, is there something more we should know about marriage? For Catholics marriage is something much greater. The Church teaches us that marriage between two baptized persons is more than a legal arrangement, more than a contract, and more than romance. Marriage is a sacrament and was raised to that dignity by Christ. In the *sacrament of Matrimony*, a baptized man and a baptized woman commit themselves to each other as partners for the whole of life. This partnership is a sacred covenant that mirrors the relationship that Christ has with the Church.

In marriage we realize in a particular way that we were created by God out of love and that men and women were meant for one another. In the very first book of the Bible, we read that God said, "It is not good for the man to be alone" (Genesis 2:18). In the Christian ideal of marriage, a man and a woman are equal partners, devoted to each other in true love, committed to each other's good, and ready to find God at the very center of their love for each other. Such a love cannot help but be open to new life—to the procreation and education of children. So important is this marriage in the Lord that the Church calls the family the domestic Church.

How does this come about? In the sacrament of Matrimony, a man and woman commit themselves totally to each other in Christ. They vow to love and help each other for the rest of their lives and to share this love with their children. Therefore the marriage covenant is a blessing and a gift to the couple, to their children, to the Church, and to the whole world.

As we shall see, this is a sacrament filled with great joy and love. But it is also a serious and solemn obligation. Not everyone is ready to make such a commitment. It takes time, hard work, and deep dedication before two people are ready to walk down the aisle of a church and speak the vows of marriage to each other. Let's explore the most important aspects of marriage from the Catholic point of view and then look at the beautiful celebration of this sacrament.

A Life-giving Sign of Grace

People are often amazed when they realize that Scripture uses the marriage covenant as a symbol of God's love for his people. God is always faithful. The prophet Hosea knew this and compared God to a faithful husband and Israel to a loving bride. These are Hosea's words:

> I will espouse you to me forever:
>   I will espouse you in right and in justice,
>   in love and in mercy;
> I will espouse you in fidelity,
>   and you shall know the LORD.
> Hosea 2:21–22

In the New Testament Jesus says: "What God has joined together, no human being must separate" (Matthew 19:6). In his letter to the Ephesians, Saint Paul compared this union of marriage to the love of Christ and the Church. Just as Christ loves his body, the Church, so husband and wife must love each other.

A sacrament is a sign given to us by Christ through which we share in God's grace—God's own life. The sacrament of Matrimony is a life-giving sign of grace, not just at the wedding ceremony when the wedding vows are made, but for the whole time of the marriage, for a lifetime during which the vows are lived out by a man and a woman.

Like each of the sacraments, the sacrament of Matrimony is a public act. Standing before God and the community of the Church, a man and woman speak vows of love and commitment. The priest or deacon who accepts these vows is the Church's official witness. There must also be two other witnesses. For a Catholic marriage to be considered valid, Catholics must marry in the presence of a priest or deacon and two witnesses. Unless otherwise dispensed, or excused, from this by the local bishop, any other marriage by Catholics would be considered invalid.

It is a surprise to many Catholics that the bride and groom themselves are the ministers of the sacrament. When the marriage vows are pronounced, the couple begins a whole new way of life. They are no longer two; they are one. The grace of this sacrament will enable them to put aside selfishness and to be open to each other in mutual support and generosity. The sacrament will strengthen them to approach an unknown future,

with its joys and sorrows. It will help them to build their family life on the rock foundation of faith in Christ. A man and woman will be able to do this only if they are ready to give themselves to each other freely in the Lord.

Getting Ready

When a couple decides to marry, it is because they have decided to spend the rest of their lives together. They become engaged and announce their intention to marry. When one or both of them is Catholic, they meet with the parish priest, deacon, or other minister to begin a time of preparation. The sacrament of Matrimony requires special preparation because this serious commitment is made for life. The couple must know of marriage's responsibilities, challenges, and graces. No one must enter into marriage lightly or without thought.

The priest or deacon will help the couple to determine whether or not they truly are free to marry to be certain that nothing or no one holds them back from making a free commitment in love. He will help them to

see that marriage vows must be made not only freely but also faithfully. When we marry, we promise fidelity to one person with a permanent commitment. We do not stand before God and the Church and say that we are only going to try this out for a while!

Most dioceses sponsor special preparation courses that are required before marriage. These are called Pre-Cana classes, reminding us of Christ's first miracle at the wedding feast in Cana of Galilee (John 2:1–11). In any event, marriage preparation takes time. Most parishes require six months' advance notice. As one parish bulletin stated: See the pastor before you rent the reception hall!

So much can go into planning the wedding celebration. But such a celebration will be empty if the bride and groom are not prepared. Marriage is a big step, perhaps the greatest step in life. If we prepare well, we will give ourselves the best chance of being successful and happy. And that is exactly what God and his Church want for us all.

Think about important events in your life that have taken preparation on your part. Why is preparation for marriage so important?

CATHOLIC ID

The banns of marriage are customary in the Church. The word *banns* means "proclamations" or "announcements." For three weeks before a wedding, the parish prints in the weekly bulletin or announces at Mass the names of the bride and groom and the date of the wedding. Because we are a community, we need to know when our sisters and brothers in faith are taking this decisive step in their lives. When you read or hear the banns of marriage, pray for those entering into this beautiful sacramental commitment.

Real Love

What is real love? Certainly the feelings of love sometimes just happen. Such feelings are natural and beautiful gifts from God. They help to make us more human, more caring of others. But a commitment to love cannot be based on feelings alone because feelings come and go. The love needed in marriage must be a love based on a firm decision, a free choice. No other love will do. But this type of love is not easy. This love keeps on loving even when things get tough and we say to ourselves, "I don't feel like it." This is the love we vow when we say, "I promise to be true to you in good times and in bad, in sickness and in health. I will love you and honor you all the days of my life."

Catholics can never take the attitude that "we can always divorce if it doesn't go well." We believe that the sacrament of Matrimony forms an *indissoluble bond*—a bond that can never be broken. Real love based in Christ is not here one day and gone the next; real love is forever. Saint Paul once wrote that real love "bears all things, believes all things, hopes all things, endures all things. Love never fails" (1 Corinthians 13:7–8).

Sadly, some people cannot make this type of commitment in Christ. Others try too early or when they are immature. Others fail to work at marriage. But such a beautiful understanding of marriage is real. Such marriages are possible.

Celebrating Matrimony

Like every other sacrament Matrimony reveals something of the paschal mystery, the death and resurrection of Christ. When two Catholics celebrate the sacrament of Matrimony, they celebrate their willingness to imitate and encounter Christ in their lives of service, in the dyings and risings, sorrows and joys of family life.

The meaning of Catholic marriage is expressed in the rite of marriage. The sacrament of Matrimony has the same basic shape as all the other sacraments: gathering, storytelling, the sacramental action (in Matrimony, the exchange of vows, preferably within the eucharistic meal), and commissioning. It is most fitting that the rite of marriage be celebrated with a nuptial Mass. In this way the bride and groom unite themselves to the self-offering of Christ in the Eucharist. It is also fitting that they receive the Body and Blood of Christ in Holy Communion, which seals their union in Christ.

Gathering The priest or deacon usually greets the bride and groom, welcoming them and their families and friends in the name of the Church.

Storytelling The couple often selects the Scripture passages from the rite that correspond to the religious meaning they wish to express in their wedding. The readings will sometimes have a reference to creation, for husband and wife are starting something new: a new relationship, a new family, a new domestic church. The readings will sometimes refer to the two becoming one. They will often refer to the unselfish love stressed by Jesus in the gospels.

Exchange of Vows It is the bride and groom who, by their free consent and mutual vows, are the ministers of the sacrament. The pledging of vows must be *witnessed* by a priest, the Church's official witness, and two other people, usually the maid of honor and the best man. The free consent of the couple and the presence of a priest and two witnesses are the essential signs of the sacrament. The bride and groom stand before the congregation and vow "to give themselves, each to the other, mutually and definitively, in order to live a covenant of faithful and fruitful love" (*Catechism*, 1662).

God is faithful "no matter what." In order for the couple to be a sign of this divine love, they must reflect God's faithful love in three ways: in *unity* of body, heart, and soul; in *indissolubility*, that is, lifelong faithfulness; and in *openness to having children.* These three qualities are essential to Christian marriage.

Meal Sharing As we have seen, when two practicing Catholics exchange their vows, they usually do so in the context of the Eucharist at a nuptial Mass. All that marriage says about union with Christ in sacrificial love is said even more eloquently in the Eucharist.

Following the Lord's Prayer the priest extends his hands over the couple and invokes the Holy Spirit upon them. The Holy Spirit is the seal of their covenant and an ever-present source of love and strength.

Commissioning The blessing at the end of Mass is directed especially to the bride and groom. One blessing asks that the peace of Christ may always be in their home, that they will live in peace with all people, and that they will always bear witness to the love of God in this world.

 Recall a wedding liturgy in which you have participated. Can you describe the main elements based on the outline given here?

Are You Ready for Marriage?

The correct answer to the question above is, of course, no. Readiness for a lifelong commitment demands a certain maturity, an ability to care for and support a family, and an awareness of the challenges and responsibilities that joining one's life to another's demands. Still most of you are, whether you know it or not, preparing for marriage right now.

As we grow through life, we become aware of our own unique characteristics. Some of these we can do nothing about. The color of our hair and eyes is based on genetics, not personal preference. Other characteristics, however, even if based on inborn tendencies, are not fixed forever. We can make decisions about our personality traits. We can decide, for example, to be kind, to be more patient, to listen to others, to keep our promises. In other words, we can begin now to decide what kind of person we want to become, what kind of interpersonal skills we want to learn.

The vocation of marriage requires interpersonal skills. Marriage is a union of two compatible but often very different people. Two unique personalities must learn to make important decisions together, to discuss their differences of opinion, to allow themselves to reveal deep feelings to the other. This is not easy for anyone!

Scripture UPDATE

The Church provides a variety of Scripture readings for the rite of marriage. Find the passages listed here. Then choose one. What does it tell you about the sacrament of Matrimony?

1 Corinthians 12:31—13:8   1 John 4:7–12
Ephesians 5:2, 25–32

The following questionnaire is a sample of the kinds of questions engaged couples are asked. Such a questionnaire can help the couple to become more aware of their own personalities and their ability to communicate with others. You have probably used these skills in friendships, in groups or teams you might belong to, or in group projects in school. Everyone needs these skills. Those who work on developing their interpersonal skills are headed toward satisfying friendships and, in time, a good marriage.

You may want to write your personal responses to these questions in your journal and then share your ideas and solutions in small groups. Check those skills you wish to improve.

My Interpersonal Skills

☐ **A**m I a good listener? How do I show this?

☐ **H**ow do I deal with criticism?

☐ **D**o I show respect for others in my speech, saying "please," "thank you," and "pardon me"?

☐ **D**o I talk over problems with the person or persons directly involved?

☐ **W**hat is my reaction when my plans are upset for some reason?

☐ **H**ave I learned to play with and watch over young children safely?

☐ **D**o I apologize when I've made a mistake or caused a problem?

☐ **D**o I spend money wisely?

☐ **H**ow do I treat the elderly persons I meet?

☐ **W**hat do I do when I am angry? How do I solve the problem?

☐ **D**o I speak with adults respectfully and courteously?

☐ **D**o I give positive feedback? Do I affirm others and thank them when I am grateful for their help or support?

☐ **D**o I look for ways to help others when I can?

☐ **I**f I have a serious problem or need, do I talk it over with an adult I can trust?

How do you think developing interpersonal skills can prepare you for marriage?

PUTTING IT TOGETHER

things to think about

What do you think makes a good marriage?

What makes a marriage Catholic? Why are the bride and groom the ministers of the sacrament?

Why does the Church urge that Catholics be married at a nuptial Mass?

things to share

Do you see any connection between the kind of friend a person is now and a vocation to married life? If so, what is it?

Of the marriages you have observed, what interpersonal skills have you noticed in use? What interpersonal skills would you look for in a marriage partner?

WORDS TO REMEMBER

Find and define the following:

sacrament of Matrimony _____
_____
_____

indissoluble bond _____
_____
_____

OnLine
WITH THE PARISH

Each parish provides some form of preparation for those who wish to marry. Some parishes put the prospective bride and groom in contact with a Catholic couple who have been living the sacrament for a number of years. Some parishes provide Pre-Cana courses or Engaged Encounter weekends. What form of preparation for marriage is provided by your parish? What does it involve?

1 What did Jesus say about marriage? What did Saint Paul write about marriage?

2 How do Catholic engaged couples prepare for the sacrament of Matrimony?

3 What are the essential signs of the sacrament of Matrimony?

4 What three qualities are essential to Christian marriage?

5 What interpersonal skills do you now have? Also name one skill that you would like to become better at. How will you do this?

Life in the Spirit

This is a prayer from the Blessing for a Family or Household. You may want to pray it for your own family.

In good times and in bad,
in sickness and in health,
we belong to each other
as we belong to you, God
   ever faithful.
By morning and by night
may your name be on our lips,
a blessing to all our days:
so may kindness and patience
   be ever among us,
a hunger for justice,
and songs of thankfulness in all
   we do.
We ask this through Christ our Lord.

Catholic Household Blessings and Prayers

Mary and the Saints

Lord, this is the people that longs to see your face.

Solemnity of All Saints

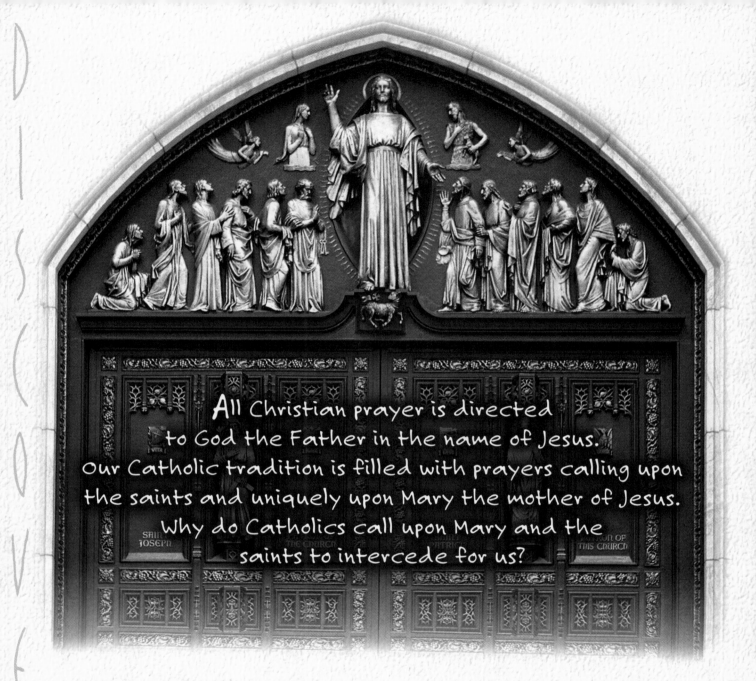

All Christian prayer is directed
to God the Father in the name of Jesus.
Our Catholic tradition is filled with prayers calling upon
the saints and uniquely upon Mary the mother of Jesus.
Why do Catholics call upon Mary and the
saints to intercede for us?

The Communion of Saints

Sometimes on headstones in a cemetery, there is a request: "Please pray for me," or "Pray for the repose of the soul of…." We find such inscriptions in the early Christian cemeteries, too.

On the tombs of the martyrs, however, the inscriptions are different: They ask the martyrs to pray for us! These inscriptions are our earliest evidence of Christian prayer to the saints. From the beginning Christians have called upon Mary and the saints to intercede with God for them.

You remember that old saying: The way we pray shows what we believe. And how do we pray about the saints? In the preface for Masses on saints' days, we thank God because:

You renew the Church in every age
by raising up men and women outstanding
   in holiness,
living witnesses of your unchanging love.
They inspire us by their heroic lives,
and help us by their constant prayers
to be the living sign of your saving power.

We honor the saints because of their example and their intercession. They show us how to follow Christ, and they help us by their prayers.

The holiness of the saints is a reflection of God's holiness. In the sacraments the Father shares his holiness with us through the Son and the Holy Spirit. Through the sacraments we enter into a "holy communion" and share, in union with the saints, God's life. Our union with God's holiness and with his holy ones (the saints) is called the *communion of saints.*

When we use the title Saint, we normally think of those men and women of exceptional holiness whose lives we see in movies or read about in books. It is important to remember that we too are called to be saints. Saint Paul, in his Letter to the Ephesians, wrote: "So then you are no longer strangers and sojourners, but you are fellow citizens with the holy ones and members of the household of God" (Ephesians 2:19).

United in Holiness

The doctrine of the communion of saints has very important consequences for our daily lives. Think of what it means—we are united with the saints in a common holiness!

For example, think of your physical body. When you exercise and strengthen your arms, your whole body benefits. When you do aerobics to strengthen your lungs and your heart, your whole body benefits. So it is with the body of Christ. "Since all the faithful form one body, the good of each is communicated to the others" (*Catechism*, 947).

Because we are members of the same body of Christ, all the good works, the merits, and the graces of the saints are communicated to us. What an encouragement this can be as we struggle and often fail in our efforts to follow Jesus. The communion of saints assures us that *together* we form one family in Christ. In the family of Christians, as in a human family, the good of one member is shared with the whole family. When your mother wins the lottery, the whole family gets rich!

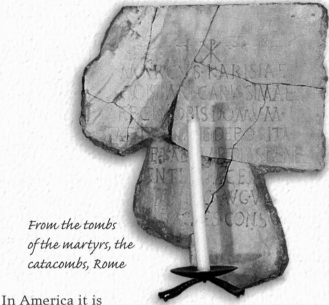

From the tombs of the martyrs, the catacombs, Rome

In America it is important to emphasize this collective or communal dimension of our salvation because our culture places great emphasis on *individual* accomplishment. This attitude, however, does not apply to salvation or holiness. When it comes to holiness and sanctity, we are all in this together. We are one body, one family, one community in Christ. God's holiness is a *shared* gift.

What, then, does holiness mean for each one of us? As individuals, we each respond to God's grace in our own way and as best we can. We grow in holiness through a continual process of turning our lives toward God. We keep trying to empty ourselves of selfishness and sin in order to allow God's Spirit to fill us and to work in us. The saints have accomplished this to such a degree that when we look at their lives, we see and understand what Saint Paul meant when he wrote, "I live, no longer I, but Christ lives in me" (Galatians 2:20).

The communion of saints is both a tremendous responsibility and a source of great hope. Our responsibility is to follow Christ faithfully, as members of his body. Our hope is that we, together with all the saints, will share eternally in his final victory.

 Do you feel you have any responsibility to build up the communion of saints? Describe it.

Celebrating the Saints

Devotion to Our Lady and the saints goes back to the earliest days of the Church. It is a rich tradition. We have seen how the liturgical year celebrates the birth, life, passion, death, and resurrection of Jesus. The liturgical year also celebrates the life of Mary and the lives of the saints.

Liturgical celebrations are divided into three degrees. The most important days are called *solemnities.* For example, the days we celebrate the Trinity, Our Lord, or the Holy Spirit—Trinity Sunday, Christmas, Easter, Pentecost—are solemnities. In addition, we celebrate eight solemnities in honor of Mary or the saints each year. These include the solemnities of Mary, the Mother of God (January 1); Joseph, patron of the universal Church (March 19); John the Baptist (June 24); and the Apostles Peter and Paul (June 29). Why would you think these celebrations are given the rank of solemnity?

Second in order of importance is that of *feast.* This rank includes, among others, the feasts of apostles and evangelists; the feast of the angels and archangels (September 29); the feast of the first martyr, Stephen (December 26); and the feast of the Holy Innocents (December 28).

The final rank is *memorial.* On memorial days we celebrate the *memory* of a saint. Just as you might mark the birthdays of your friends on your calendar, the Church marks the birthdays of individual saints. However, there is one important difference. The Church does not celebrate the day the saints were born on earth but marks instead the day on which they were born into eternal life—that is, the day on which they died. It is their passage into new and eternal life that we celebrate, affirming that Christ's victory over death became fully real in their lives.

Blessed Katharine Drexel

Saint Frances Xavier Cabrini

Reflections of the Holy

What does it mean when we call someone a *saint*? The word means "holy." In order to understand the holiness of the saints, we must start with the realization that only God is holy. We pray in the Glory to God at Mass:

For you alone are the Holy One,
you alone are the Lord,
you alone are the Most High,
Jesus Christ….

If we call anyone other than God "holy," it is because this person reflects God's holiness. When we honor a saint's achievements, we are not honoring what the saint did; rather, we are honoring what God did through the saint. Holiness is achieved, not by doing great things, but by allowing God's greatness to work in us.

The Church is aware that millions and millions of Christians have lived holy lives and that they now share in the happiness of God's life in heaven. These are all saints in the general sense of the word. However, in order to recognize the holiness of particular saints in a formal way, the Church has instituted the process called *canonization.* In order for a holy person to be canonized, an expert in Church matters must study the holy person's life.

Saint Charles Lwanga

After this report of faith and good works is given to the bishop, more investigation is done. The final results are then sent to the Congregation for the Causes of Saints in Rome. The holy person may then be beatified and given the title of "Blessed."

Usually, three miracles (often healings of the sick) attributed to the holy person's intercession are required before formal declaration of sainthood. Then the pope, in a beautiful and solemn ceremony, canonizes the saint, declaring that this holy person is truly a saint and extending veneration of this newly canonized saint to the whole Church.

Each year we celebrate well-known saints—saints such as Saint Francis of Assisi, Saint Thérèse of Lisieux, Saint Joseph, and the special patron saint of our diocese or parish. We also celebrate those saints who worked for God and his people on American soil: Blessed Kateri Tekakwitha, Saint Isaac Jogues and the North American Martyrs, Saint Elizabeth Ann Seton, Saint John Neumann, Saint Frances Xavier Cabrini, and Blessed Katharine Drexel.

Pope John Paul II has added a large number of saints and "blesseds" to the Church's calendar. They include the Vietnamese martyrs Saint Andrew Dung-Lac and Companions; the Korean martyrs Saints Andrew Kim, Paul Chong and Companions; and Blessed Juan Diego, the native Mexican who was privileged with the vision of Our Lady of Guadalupe. The previous pope, Pope Paul VI, canonized the martyrs of Uganda, Saint Charles Lwanga and Companions. Celebrating the saints reminds us that holiness is not restricted to one time or place. Saints come from all over the world.

The diversity in the lives of the saints teaches us that all Christians are called to holiness by imitating Christ in their particular circumstances. Often, by learning the life stories of the saints, we find that they faced spiritual challenges similar to the ones we face in our own lives. As we learn from them, these great heroes and heroines become our role models in the Christian life.

Blessed
Juan Diego

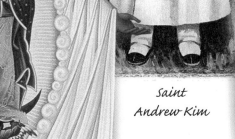

Saint
Andrew Kim

Blessed
Kateri Tekakwitha

Some of the many cultural representations of the Blessed Virgin Mary in art

Mary, Mother of Jesus

Throughout this book we have emphasized that our prayers, sacraments, and devotions begin and end with Jesus Christ, the Son of the Father. We must never lose sight of this most basic fact. But through the centuries those who have loved and served Jesus have also shown a love and devotion to Mary, his mother. Mary is the first of the disciples and the model for all Christians.

Mary has been honored in many ways through the centuries. However, everything that can be said about Mary, all the honor given to her, is due to two important facts: She is the mother of Jesus, and she is his first disciple. By understanding these two relationships, we can understand the role Mary plays in our salvation and in our devotion.

First of all, we honor Mary because of her relationship to Jesus: She is his mother. Mary does not draw our attention to herself; she always points to Jesus. Each of the honors given to Mary is best understood in relation to Christ. We can see this in the four principal privileges for which the Church

has traditionally honored Mary: Mother of God, Virgin, the Immaculate Conception, and the Assumption.

What we believe about Mary is based on our understanding of Jesus. For example, when the second Council of Ephesus (A.D. 431) proclaimed Mary the Mother of God, it was discussing who *Jesus* was. The child that Mary bore in her womb was divine and therefore Mary, the mother of that child, is indeed the Mother of God. The title *Mother of God* is a statement about Mary, about her first and greatest privilege, but it is first and foremost a statement about Jesus. We celebrate the Solemnity of Mary, Mother of God on January 1.

We call Mary *Virgin* because the Church has always believed and taught that Jesus was conceived by the power of the Holy Spirit.

Because God chose Mary to be the Mother of the Savior, it is fitting that she was the first to be saved. We believe that she was redeemed and free from all sin from the very beginning of her life—that is, from the moment of her conception.

We call this privilege the *immaculate conception.* We celebrate the Solemnity of the Immaculate Conception on December 8.

We believe that when Mary's life on earth was over, God took her into heaven body and soul. This participation in the resurrection and ascension of her son is called the *assumption* of the Blessed Virgin. We celebrate the Solemnity of the Assumption on August 15.

Mary, First Disciple of Jesus

The second reason we honor Mary is her relation to the Church: Mary is the first member of the Church, the model disciple. Genuine devotion to Mary is balanced between Mary, Mother of God and Mary, the model disciple. The first emphasizes God's choice; the second emphasizes Mary's response.

What does it mean to be a disciple? To be a disciple of Jesus, we must follow his example in doing the will of his Father. Jesus taught us to pray "Your will be done." Jesus himself was a perfect example of this prayer. Throughout his life, from birth to death, he did the will of his Father.

In the garden, on the night before his death on the cross, Jesus prayed, "Father, if you are willing, take this cup away from me; still, not my will but yours be done" (Luke 22:42). The prayer of Christ's disciples must be this same prayer: "Not my will but yours be done."

No one has prayed this or lived this more perfectly than Mary. When the angel asked her to become the Mother of God, she replied, "May it be done to me according to your word" (Luke 1:38). Because Mary listened so carefully to the word of God, she is able to help us listen to God's word in our own lives. As Mary helped others listen to Jesus, she can help us listen to him, too. At the wedding at Cana, it was Mary who noticed that the wine was running out. After she

told Jesus about this, she instructed the servants, "Do whatever he tells you" (John 2:5). They listened to Jesus, did as he asked, and the water became wine. The miracle at Cana began with Mary. Mary shows herself to be the perfect disciple—one who, like Jesus, always seeks the will of God.

In her discipleship Mary is an ideal for each of us. She is all that the Church is and hopes to be. We are the Church. We, too, are disciples. Mary, as Mother of God, bore Jesus in her womb and gave him birth. Today we, the Church, bear Christ in our bodies by Baptism and Eucharist. We are to bring forth Christ to our world by word and example. This is how we live as Jesus' disciples. Mary's virginity is the model for our own single-minded devotion to Christ. Mary's sinlessness is a model for the Church. Mary's assumption into heaven is also our destiny as disciples of Jesus.

 What does Mary's life say to you about discipleship?

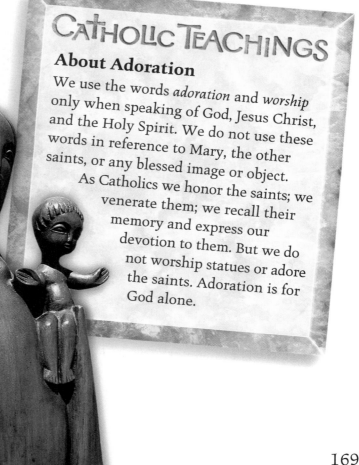

CATHOLIC TEACHINGS

About Adoration

We use the words *adoration* and *worship* only when speaking of God, Jesus Christ, and the Holy Spirit. We do not use these words in reference to Mary, the other saints, or any blessed image or object. As Catholics we honor the saints; we venerate them; we recall their memory and express our devotion to them. But we do not worship statues or adore the saints. Adoration is for God alone.

> Hail Mary, full of grace,
> the Lord is with you!
> Blessed are you among women,
> and blessed is the fruit of your
> womb, Jesus.
> Holy Mary, Mother of God,
> pray for us sinners,
> now and at the hour of our death.
> Amen.

The greeting "Shout for joy" is addressed not only to Mary but also to us. And why? Because the Lord is with us, too, in our midst. The presence of the Lord fills Mary—and us—with favor, blessing, and grace.

The second greeting of the Hail Mary is that of Elizabeth: "Most blessed are you among women, and blessed is the fruit of your womb" (Luke 1:42). Mary is always seen in relation to her son. As Jesus is the source of every blessing, Mary, who bore Jesus in her womb and brought him forth to the world, is indeed worthy to be called blessed. She is the model and example for us all. For we, by our acceptance of God's will in our lives, show Christ to our world. We too become both blessed and a source of blessing.

The Hail Mary

The most common prayer to Mary, the one all Catholics know by heart, is the Hail Mary.

The prayer consists of two greetings and a petition. The two greetings are taken from the first chapter of Luke's Gospel. The first is the greeting of the angel Gabriel (Luke 1:28); the second, that of Mary's cousin Elizabeth (Luke 1:42).

The greeting of the angel Gabriel reminds us of the Book of Zephaniah: "Shout for joy, O daughter Zion! . . . The LORD your God is in your midst" (Zephaniah 3:14, 17). In the Hail Mary we pray, "Hail Mary, full of grace, the Lord is with you." The word we translate as "Hail" is the same word Zephaniah used: "Rejoice" or "Shout for joy." In Gabriel's greeting to Mary, it is as if he were saying to her, "Shout for joy, O highly favored one! The Lord is in your midst." When we say "Hail Mary," then, it is helpful to remember that this greeting is a joyful reminder of God's goodness and favor: Shout for joy!

The Visitation (detail), Domenico Ghirlandaio, 1491

The second half of the Hail Mary is a traditional prayer of petition whose origins are lost in history. In it we ask that Mary will intercede for us "now and at the hour of our death."

It is important to remember that, when we call upon Mary and the saints, we are asking them to pray for us, to intercede with God for us. All prayer is ultimately addressed to God—the Father, the Son, and the Holy Spirit. When we ask the intercession of Mary and the saints, we are not "going around" God at all. In placing our needs before Our Lady and the saints, we are asking them to present our needs to God, the source of all good.

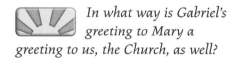 *In what way is Gabriel's greeting to Mary a greeting to us, the Church, as well?*

The Rosary

There came a time when many Christians no longer knew the psalms by heart, so they began to meditate on the life of Jesus while reciting the Hail Mary or the Lord's Prayer. Eventually this practice was called praying the rosary. By the fifteenth century it had become a popular devotion.

The rosary can be prayed alone or with others. Usually we start with the Apostles' Creed, one Our Father, three Hail Marys, and one Glory to the Father. Following this introduction, we begin our meditation on the mysteries. Meditation—thinking and praying about the wonderful events of our salvation—is at the very heart of the rosary.

Each decade of the rosary is made up of one Our Father, ten Hail Marys, and one Glory to the Father. At the beginning of each decade, we select the

Scripture UPDATE

Most of the mysteries of the rosary come from the gospel accounts in the Scripture. The *joyful mysteries* are the annunciation, visitation, nativity, presentation, and finding in the temple. The *sorrowful mysteries* are the agony in the garden, scourging, crowning with thorns, carrying of the cross, and crucifixion. The *glorious mysteries* are the resurrection, ascension, descent of the Holy Spirit, assumption of Mary, and coronation of Mary. These last two mysteries are based on tradition.

These mysteries are not obligatory. We are free to meditate on any mystery or event in the life of Jesus or his mother. We need not pray all five decades of the rosary at once. Some Catholics carry the rosary with them and pray a few decades when they can during the day. Some families pray the rosary at the beginning of a car trip. It is a common practice to pray the rosary before going to sleep.

mystery on which we are going to meditate. Then we think of this event in the life of Jesus or in the life of his mother while praying the ten Hail Marys. We usually end the Rosary with a centuries-old prayer to Mary, the Hail, Holy Queen.

 Say a decade of the rosary now. Choose a mystery for meditation, and end the decade by praying the Hail, Holy Queen.

PUTTING IT TOGETHER

things to think about

What does it mean to be a saint?

Why do you think the Church brings the lives of the saints before us each year?

What does the life of Mary teach you about being a disciple of Jesus?

things to share

What difference should the communion of saints make in our lives as Catholics?

What is your favorite Scripture story about Mary?

WORDS TO REMEMBER

Find and define the following:

immaculate conception _____
_____
_____

communion of saints _____
_____
_____

OnLine WITH THE PARISH

Each parish church has a "title;" that is, it is named after the Trinity or Our Lord (or a mystery in his life), the Holy Spirit, the Blessed Virgin Mary, one of the angels, or a saint. What is the title of your parish church? When is this title celebrated? What special things are done on that day?

Some parishes offer a calendar to parishioners each year. On this calendar are marked all the saints' days. Look up your birthday. What saint shares this day with you?

Describe the three levels of liturgical celebration.

1

How do we become holy?

2

What happens in the process of canonization?

3

Name and explain one of the four principal privileges for which the Church honors the Blessed Mother.

4

What is the prayer of petition in the Hail Mary?

5

Life in the Spirit

It has long been a Catholic custom to honor Mary by naming special places for her. The original name of Los Angeles, for example, is Nuestra Señora de los Angeles, "Our Lady of the Angels." Sometimes places, usually churches or religious houses, are named both in honor of Mary and in gratitude for one of God's gifts in her, as in her titles, Queen of Heaven or Mother of God.

Find the Litany of the Blessed Virgin Mary on page 188. Each invocation calls on Mary using one of her special titles. Pray the litany now together. If possible, share it and pray it with your family.

CHAPTER 15

Paths of Prayer

You will show me the path to life,
abounding joy in your presence.
Psalm 16:11

Prayer is a path that leads
to God; prayer is a window that reflects
God's light; prayer is a heart open to God's love.
What is prayer for you?

Windows of Prayer

In *prayer* we raise our hearts and minds to God. We ask God for the good things we need, we thank him for his gifts, we express our sorrow for sin, we pray for others, and we praise him for his goodness. With the help of the Holy Spirit and the tradition of the Church, we can pray in many ways. Here is one you might like to try.

We have seen them all of our lives: beautiful stained-glass windows, carefully crafted filters of light and color. We are drawn to them. Why? Because they help us to raise our hearts and minds to God.

The most famous and beautiful windows are called rose windows. They are circular. The circle is an ancient symbol of God and of eternity. Their interior panes fold out from the center like the petals of a rose. The rose window invites us to travel its paths and then to focus on the center.

Look at the empty stained-glass window here. How would you complete it? Here is a suggestion: Make this window into an expression of your relationship with God. Like a stained-glass window, this relationship has many dimensions. Think about the sacraments you have celebrated; you may want to symbolize each one in a section of your window. Think about your times of prayer, both during the liturgy and alone. These could be symbolized in sections of your window. How do family and friends help you find God? Symbolize this in your window. Perhaps the Scriptures will find a place in your window as well.

The center of a stained-glass window is very important. Everything else in the window revolves around it. Sometimes the center of the window holds a picture or icon of Jesus or Mary. Sometimes the center is a circle of color. Sometimes it holds a cross, or a triangle to symbolize the Trinity. What would you put in the center of your window? Perhaps you might insert a symbol of Jesus: the cross as symbol of the paschal mystery or bread and wine, the symbols of the Eucharist. What symbolizes the center of your relationship with God?

Although stained-glass windows are works of art, they are not usually given titles. However, you may want to title yours. A title summarizes the meaning of a work. Choose a title to summarize the meaning of your stained-glass window.

Imagine that your window is one of the windows in a great cathedral. Act as a tour guide to explain the meaning of your window, section by section, to the group.

JOURNAL

Use your stained-glass window as a window of prayer and reflection. Beginning with the center, write a short prayer expressing the meaning of each section of the window. If one section symbolizes your Baptism, you might write a prayer like this: "Thank you, God our Father, for choosing me as one of your children. Thank you, Jesus Christ our Lord, for saving me and showing me the way. Thank you, Holy Spirit, for guiding my path. All praise to you! Amen."

Praying with Scripture

The Sacred Scriptures can enrich our prayer immensely. They are the "faith record" of God's mysterious plan—what God has done in history and the revelation of God's plan for the world. A good way to pray is to take the Bible, read a passage, and then talk it over with God.

Praying with just one or two Scripture verses is a traditional and practical way to make prayer a part of our everyday lives. We can easily pray a short, easy-to-remember Scripture verse at work or play or during those "between times" we find ourselves in so often: between home and school, between lunch and recess, between the ending of one class and the beginning of another.

Here are several ways to pray with Scripture. Which appeal to you?

The Our Father

The whole gospel of Jesus Christ is summed up in the Our Father. It is the purest and most essential prayer of the Church. When we pray the Our Father, we pray with the attitude of Jesus and the Spirit of Jesus. We pray for what Jesus wants—that God's will be done on earth. As we pray the Our Father, we become one with Jesus and one with the Father in love and trust. The Our Father can be found in Matthew 6:9–13 and in Luke 11:2–4.

Scripture Pictures

When people asked Saint Ignatius Loyola for help in prayer, he advised them to picture a scene from Scripture and to put themselves into the scene. Try it with Matthew 8:23–27. Imagine the people, the sounds, the smells; and especially, see Jesus as he speaks and acts. What is he saying to you? When you finish, write your thoughts in your journal.

God's Word for the Day

Compile a list of at least seven favorite Scripture passages. Choose one each day as your special verse. Every time your mind is free or you are between activities, recall your verse and say it to yourself a few times. Here are two for your list:

- "Your word is a lamp for my feet, a light for my path" (Psalm 119:105).
- "I am the good shepherd, and I know mine and mine know me" (John 10:14).

Today's Scripture

Using the Church's calendar of Scripture readings, find the readings for today. Read them and the psalm carefully. If you find a verse or idea meaningful, stop and let it sink in. Stay with it as long as you like. Then go on. Choose one of the verses, and recall it often during the day.

Scripture and Music

Music is a traditional and beautiful way to focus on the words and meaning of Scripture. Try setting a favorite verse to a simple melody, perhaps in a chantlike style. Create a harmony as well! You may want to use a Scripture story or set of verses as the basis for an entire song. Saint John Chrysostom wrote many Scripture hymns for the Church. Ask his help!

Scripture Exchange

Spend some time looking through the New Testament. Write down, on an index card or a slip of paper, one or two verses you like. Collect them from the group in a box or basket. Then invite each group member to draw one. You may want to decorate or illustrate your verse on paper and display it.

The Prayer of the Name

"You shall name him Jesus" (Luke 1:31). The name of Jesus is a simple but powerful prayer, and using the holy name of Jesus in prayer is an ancient tradition in the Church. Begin by closing your eyes and becoming still. Breathe slowly and deeply. Then, as you breathe in, quietly say "Jesus." As you breathe out, you may want to say "Savior" or "peace" or another word that reminds you of Jesus. Continue this rhythm for as long as you wish.

An illuminated page of Gregorian chant, late fourteenth century

With or Without Words

In our Catholic life of prayer, we often pray with words, aloud, and usually with others. This prayer with words is called *vocal prayer* because we pray not only with our minds and hearts but with our voices as well. The prayers we say during the liturgy are vocal prayers, as are traditional prayers such as the Our Father and the Hail Mary.

There are many paths to God in prayer. Vocal prayer is one of them. Once two sisters asked Saint Teresa of Avila how to find union with God. "Say the Our Father," responded Teresa. Sometimes when we say a familiar prayer carefully and thoughtfully, we gain insight into the meaning of the words. Then the words slowly fade away, and we find ourselves "just being" at peace in God. This is the prayer of contemplation.

Contemplation is the prayer of union with God. We might also call it the prayer of "just being with" God. If you look up the word *contemplation* in the dictionary, you will find: "the act of looking at attentively and thoughtfully." The prayer of contemplation is simply looking at God. As one saint described this kind of prayer, "I look at God and he looks at me."

Another path to union with God is praying with the words of Scripture, as we have seen. If we keep a special Scripture verse in mind during the day, we may find a new meaning in it. Or simply saying the words of Scripture quietly and peacefully can lead us to "just being with" God.

The path of meditation is another path to union with God. *Meditation* is simply "thinking about God," and it can easily flow into "being with" God. Most often we meditate on the Scriptures, but other spiritual books can be starting points as well, especially those that explain the Scriptures and inspire us to live the Christian life. For now, let's choose a Scripture passage, Mark 10:46–52, for our meditation.

A Scripture Meditation

Before meditating, it is a good idea to help yourself become calm, peaceful, and undistracted. Sometimes listening to soft background music can help. First sit in a straight but comfortable position and close your eyes. Now let's try it.

Imagine yourself sitting by the side of a dusty road. You look down the road. You are waiting for Jesus to come by. Already you see him in the distance, surrounded by a large crowd.

Suddenly, across the road, you notice someone— Bartimaeus, a blind man. He, too, is waiting for Jesus. You hear him call out, "Jesus, Son of David, have pity on me." Jesus and the crowd are coming closer. What do you hear? There is the calling of Bartimaeus, the buzz of the crowd, and someone scolding Bartimaeus: "Quiet, blind man!" What do you see? There is Jesus, coming down the road. There is Bartimaeus, alone and poor, the hot sun beating down on him.

Suddenly all is silent. Jesus is here—just a few feet away. "Call him," Jesus says. Someone runs to where Bartimaeus sits in the sun. "Take courage; get up, he is calling you."

Everything is happening right in front of you. You see Bartimaeus as he joyfully throws aside his cloak, springs to his feet, and comes to Jesus. You hear Jesus ask, "What do you want me to do for you?" Bartimaeus replies in a pleading voice, "Master, I want to see." Jesus tells him, "Go your way; your faith has saved you." Immediately Bartimaeus receives his sight and begins to follow Jesus.

But wait! Jesus is stopping again. He has seen you sitting there in your special place. Jesus calls to you, "Come here, my friend." You quickly stand up and go to meet him. Jesus looks at you with great love. "So—why were you waiting for me? What do you want me to do for you?"

Think a moment. What is your answer? What does Jesus say to you?

Take time to "just be with" Jesus a little while.

Now begin to say good-bye. Watch Jesus a moment as he turns to continue his journey of healing. Now begin your own journey back. Say good-bye to your special place. Then open your eyes slowly. Let us pray the Our Father together.

LOOKING BACK

Think for a moment about your experience. If there is anything about your meditation that you would like to remember, write it in your journal now.

Did your meditation (thinking about God) flow into contemplation ("just being with" God)? If not, there is no cause for concern. In prayer God always gives us exactly what we need. All prayer—vocal prayer, meditation, and contemplation—is a gift of God's life and grace. We need only take time to receive it.

Times for Prayer

Jesus told the disciples that it is necessary to pray "always" (Luke 18:1). How is that possible? How would we ever get anything else done? One thing is certain: We will never be able to pray *at all times* unless we learn how to pray *at specific times*, times that we consciously pick out and set aside for prayer.

Certain times seem natural for prayer. All beginnings are good times for prayer, especially the beginning of each new day. As the light of the sun changes night into day, we are reminded of the light of Christ, which changes our night of doubt and uncertainty into a new day of hope and confidence in his victory. Each day is a gift. Each day is a day of Easter hope. Let us pray!

Other beginnings are also good times for prayer. It is good to pray at the beginning of a test, when you start your homework, at the beginning of a ball game, or each time you sit down to practice the piano. Some families pray together each time they begin a car trip.

The beginning of a meal is a traditional time for prayer. In a country where food is so plentiful, we sometimes forget that food is God's gift. Mealtimes are appropriate times to thank God for life and food, for family and friendship.

Grace before and after meals is an excellent time for spontaneous family prayer. As we gather at table, we remember one another's needs before God: "God, we thank you for this food. We ask you to bless Mom during these next days on her business trip. Help Tim as he studies for his history test tomorrow. Bless us all, keep us safe in this life, and welcome us in the next. Amen."

During Lent-Easter and Advent-Christmas time, the family meal can be an occasion for prayers that correspond to the liturgical season. During Advent the beginning of the evening meal is a good time to light the family Advent wreath.

Endings are also good times for prayer. As each day ends, we thank God for all that has happened during the day. The ending of the day also has an

association with the ending of our lives. Thinking about death should not be grim or scary. The paschal victory of Christ assures us that the death of the body is the beginning of eternal life, and so even this aspect of evening is related to thanksgiving.

Many Christians, as they go to bed, use the moments before falling asleep to think over the past day, to "examine their conscience," and to ask pardon for any sins they have committed during the day. Seeing each day in the perspective of eternity puts the day's troubles in perspective.

Whatever times we pick to pray, it is important to establish an *association*, to connect a time or activity with praying, so that we get into a habit of prayer. Saying a prayer each time you start your homework is not a guarantee of great grades (though it couldn't hurt!), but it will help establish a habit. Unless you get in the habit of praying regularly, at set times, you may end up not praying at all.

Sacramentals

Sacramentals are part of our daily lives. They are blessings, actions, and objects that the Church uses to prepare us for the graces of the sacraments. By objects, we mean things such as statues, medals, rosaries, candles, and crucifixes. By actions, we mean actions such as the sign of the cross, the laying on of hands, the sprinkling of blessed water. Blessings include the blessing of people, places, food, and objects. We bless ashes on Ash Wednesday and palms on Palm Sunday. Can you think of other times when we use blessings?

Unlike sacraments, which were instituted by Christ, sacramentals were instituted by the Church. The Church teaches us that sacramentals are never to be used in a magical or superstitious way or looked upon as good luck charms.

What sacramentals are part of your everyday life? You may want to write your own prayer, asking God's blessing on yourself, your family, your home, and your everyday activities.

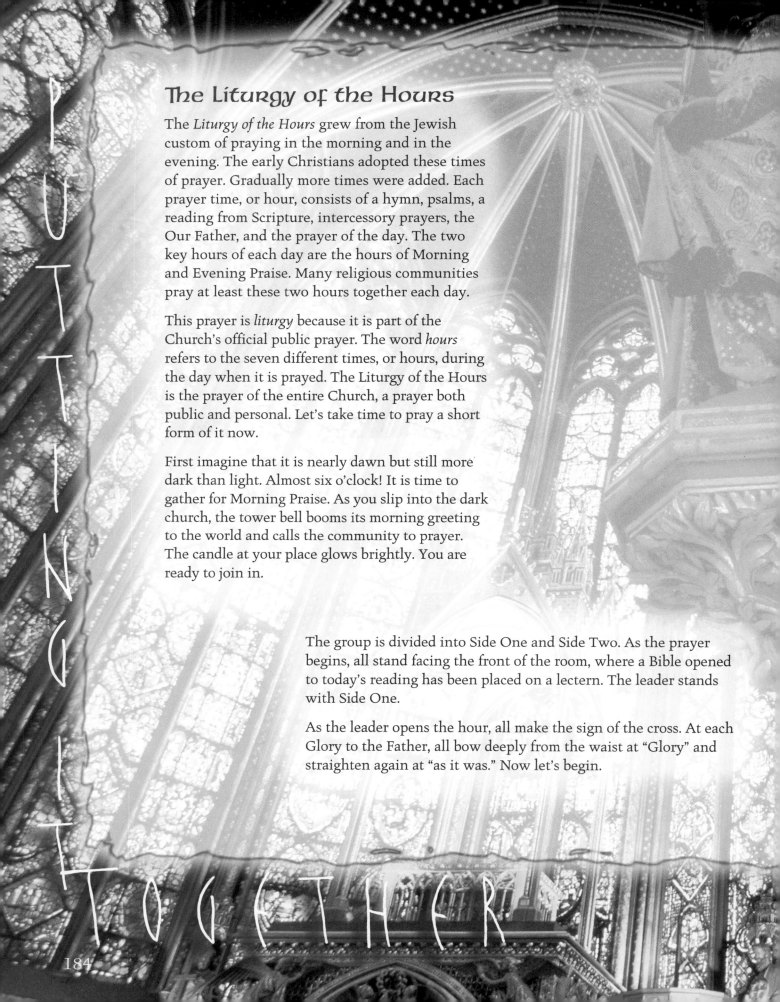

The Liturgy of the Hours

The *Liturgy of the Hours* grew from the Jewish custom of praying in the morning and in the evening. The early Christians adopted these times of prayer. Gradually more times were added. Each prayer time, or hour, consists of a hymn, psalms, a reading from Scripture, intercessory prayers, the Our Father, and the prayer of the day. The two key hours of each day are the hours of Morning and Evening Praise. Many religious communities pray at least these two hours together each day.

This prayer is *liturgy* because it is part of the Church's official public prayer. The word *hours* refers to the seven different times, or hours, during the day when it is prayed. The Liturgy of the Hours is the prayer of the entire Church, a prayer both public and personal. Let's take time to pray a short form of it now.

First imagine that it is nearly dawn but still more dark than light. Almost six o'clock! It is time to gather for Morning Praise. As you slip into the dark church, the tower bell booms its morning greeting to the world and calls the community to prayer. The candle at your place glows brightly. You are ready to join in.

The group is divided into Side One and Side Two. As the prayer begins, all stand facing the front of the room, where a Bible opened to today's reading has been placed on a lectern. The leader stands with Side One.

As the leader opens the hour, all make the sign of the cross. At each Glory to the Father, all bow deeply from the waist at "Glory" and straighten again at "as it was." Now let's begin.

PUTTING IT

TOGETHER

Morning Praise

Leader: O God, come to my assistance.

All: Lord, make haste to help me.

Side One: Glory to the Father, and to the Son, and to the Holy Spirit:

Side Two: as it was in the beginning, is now, and will be for ever. Amen.

(*All* sit *in chairs facing each other to pray Psalm 98.*)

Leader: Sing a new song to the LORD,

One: who has done marvelous deeds,

Two: Whose right hand and holy arm have won the victory.

One: The LORD has made his victory known; has revealed his triumph for the nations to see,

Two: Has remembered faithful love toward the house of Israel.

One: All the ends of the earth have seen the victory of our God.

Two: Shout with joy to the LORD, all the earth; break into song; sing praise.

One: Sing praise to the LORD with the harp, with the harp and melodious song.

Two: With trumpets and the sound of the horn shout with joy to the King, the LORD.

One: Let the sea and what fills it resound, the world and those who dwell there.

Two: Let the rivers clap their hands, the mountains shout with them for joy,

One: Before the LORD who comes, who comes to govern the earth,

Two: To govern the world with justice and the peoples with fairness.

(*All* stand *and* bow.)

One: Glory to the Father . . .

Two: as it was in the beginning . . . .

(*All* sit *for the reading.*)

Reader: A reading from the letter to the Romans (8:14–16). (*Conclude with,* "The word of the Lord.")

All: Thanks be to God.

(*All* stand *facing the lectern.*)

Leader: Let us pray as Jesus taught us: Our Father

All: who art in heaven . . . . but deliver us from evil. Amen.

Leader: May the Lord bless us, protect us from all evil and bring us to everlasting life.

All: Amen.

(*All* bow *toward the word of God.*)

With your right thumb,
trace a small cross on your lips and say:

LORD, OPEN MY LIPS,

AND MY MOUTH WILL

proclaim your praise.

UPON WAKING

GLORY TO THE FATHER,

AND TO THE SON,

and to the Holy Spirit:
as it was in the beginning, is now,
and will be for ever.
Amen.

GLORY TO THE FATHER

OUR FATHER,

WHO ART IN HEAVEN,

hallowed be thy name;
thy kingdom come;
thy will be done on earth as it is
in heaven.
Give us this day our daily bread;
and forgive us our trespasses
as we forgive those who trespass
against us;
and lead us not into temptation,
but deliver us from evil.
Amen.

OUR FATHER

WE BELIEVE
IN ONE GOD,

THE FATHER, THE ALMIGHTY,

maker of heaven and earth,
of all that is seen and unseen.

We believe in one Lord, Jesus Christ,
the only Son of God,
eternally begotten of the Father,
God from God, Light from Light,
true God from true God,
begotten, not made, one in Being
with the Father.
Through him all things were made.
For us men and for our salvation
he came down from heaven:

by the power of the Holy Spirit
he was born of the Virgin Mary,
and became man.

For our sake he was crucified under
Pontius Pilate;
he suffered, died, and was buried.
On the third day he rose again
in fulfillment of the Scriptures;
he ascended into heaven
and is seated at the right hand of
the Father.
He will come again in glory to judge the
living and the dead,
and his kingdom will have no end.

We believe in the Holy Spirit, the Lord,
the giver of life,
who proceeds from the Father
and the Son.
With the Father and the Son he is
worshiped and glorified.
He has spoken through the Prophets.
We believe in one holy catholic and
apostolic Church.
We acknowledge one baptism for the
forgiveness of sins.
We look for the resurrection of the dead,
and the life of the world to come.
Amen.

THE NICENE CREED

Blessed Be God.
Blessed Be His Holy Name.

Blessed be Jesus Christ, true God
and true man.

Blessed be the name of Jesus.

Blessed be his most sacred heart.

Blessed be his most precious blood.

Blessed be Jesus in the most holy
sacrament of the altar.

Blessed be the Holy Spirit, the Paraclete.

Blessed be the great mother of God,
Mary most holy.

Blessed be her holy and immaculate
conception.

Blessed be her glorious assumption.

Blessed be the name of Mary, virgin
and mother.

Blessed be Saint Joseph, her most chaste
spouse.

Blessed be God in his angels and in his
saints.

THE DIVINE PRAISES

Come, Holy Spirit,
Fill The Hearts of Your Faithful.

And kindle in them the fire of your love.

Send forth your Spirit and they shall be created.
And you will renew the face of the earth.

Let us pray.

Lord,
by the light of the Holy Spirit
you have taught the hearts of your faithful.
In the same Spirit
help us to relish what is right
and always rejoice in your consolation.

We ask this through Christ our Lord.
Amen.

PRAYER TO THE HOLY SPIRIT

My God,
I am Sorry for my Sins
With All My Heart.

In choosing to do wrong
and failing to do good,
I have sinned against you
whom I should love above all things.
I firmly intend, with your help,
to do penance,
to sin no more,
and to avoid whatever leads me to sin.
Our Savior Jesus Christ
suffered and died for us.
In his name, my God, have mercy.

ACT OF CONTRITION

Eternal Rest
Grant Unto Them,

O Lord.

And let perpetual light shine upon them.
May they rest in peace.
Amen.

May their souls and the souls of all the
faithful departed, through the mercy of
God, rest in peace.
Amen.

May the angels lead you into paradise;
may the martyrs come to welcome you
and take you to the holy city,
the new and eternal Jerusalem.

PRAYERS FOR THE DECEASED
FROM THE ORDER OF
CHRISTIAN FUNERALS

HAIL MARY, FULL OF GRACE,
THE LORD IS WITH YOU!

Blessed are you among women,
and blessed is the fruit of your womb, Jesus.
Holy Mary, Mother of God,
pray for us sinners,
now and at the hour of our death.
Amen.

HAIL MARY

THE ANGEL SPOKE
GOD'S MESSAGE TO MARY,

and she conceived of the Holy Spirit.
Hail Mary. . . .

"I am the lowly servant of the Lord:
let it be done to me according to your word."
Hail Mary. . . .

And the Word became flesh
and lived among us.
Hail Mary. . . .

Pray for us, holy Mother of God,
that we may become worthy of the
promises of Christ.

Let us pray.

Lord,
fill our hearts with your grace:
once, through the message of an angel you
revealed to us the incarnation of your Son;
now, through his suffering and death
lead us to the glory of his resurrection.

We ask this through Christ our Lord.
Amen.

THE ANGELUS

*The response to each
special title is "Pray for us."*

HOLY MARY
HOLY MOTHER OF GOD

Most honored of virgins

Mother of Christ
Mother of the Church
Mother of divine grace
Mother of our Creator
Mother of our Savior

Cause of our joy
Shrine of the Spirit
Health of the sick
Refuge of sinners
Comfort of the troubled
Help of Christians

Queen of angels
Queen of apostles and martyrs
Queen of all saints
Queen conceived without sin
Queen assumed into heaven
Queen of the rosary
Queen of peace

Pray for us, holy Mother of God.
That we may become worthy of
the promises of Christ.

SELECTIONS FROM THE LITANY
OF THE BLESSED VIRGIN MARY

HAIL, HOLY QUEEN,
MOTHER OF MERCY,

hail, our life, our sweetness, and our hope.
To you we cry, the children of Eve;
to you we send up our sighs,
mourning and weeping in this land of exile.
Turn, then, most gracious advocate,
your eyes of mercy toward us;
lead us home at last
and show us the blessed fruit of your
womb, Jesus:
O clement, O loving, O sweet Virgin Mary.

HAIL HOLY QUEEN

188

LORD, HAVE MERCY **LORD, HAVE MERCY**
CHRIST, HAVE MERCY CHRIST, HAVE MERCY
LORD, HAVE MERCY LORD, HAVE MERCY

Holy Mary, Mother of God	pray for us
Saint Michael	pray for us
Saint Joseph	pray for us
Saint Peter and Saint Paul	pray for us
Saint Mary Magdalene	pray for us
Saint Augustine	pray for us
Saint Benedict	pray for us
Saint Francis and Saint Dominic	pray for us
Saint Teresa	pray for us
All holy men and women	pray for us

SELECTIONS FROM THE LITANY OF THE SAINTS

THE STATIONS OF THE CROSS

1. Jesus is condemned to die.
2. Jesus takes up his cross.
3. Jesus falls the first time.
4. Jesus meets his mother.
5. Simon helps Jesus carry his cross.
6. Veronica wipes the face of Jesus.
7. Jesus falls the second time.
8. Jesus meets the women of Jerusalem.
9. Jesus falls the third time.
10. Jesus is stripped of his garments.
11. Jesus is nailed to the cross.
12. Jesus dies on the cross.
13. Jesus is taken down from the cross.
14. Jesus is laid in the tomb.

JESUS, YOU ARE GOD-WITH-US,

especially in this sacrament
of the Eucharist.
You love me as I am
and help me grow.

Come and be with me
in all my joys and sorrows.
Help me share your peace and love
with everyone I meet.

PRAYER BEFORE COMMUNION

JESUS, SON OF GOD, THANKS AND PRAISE TO YOU.

Jesus, Good Shepherd,
   thanks and praise to you.
Jesus, Lamb of God,
   thanks and praise to you.
Jesus, Bread of life and love,
   thanks and praise to you.
Jesus, Source of strength and joy,
   thanks and praise to you.

Thank you, Jesus, for your life
in mine. Help me live your good
news of love and peace.

PRAYER AFTER COMMUNION

HOLY DAYS OF OBLIGATION

SOLEMNITY OF MARY, MOTHER OF GOD
(January 1)

ALL SAINTS DAY
(November 1)

ASCENSION
(during the Easter season)

IMMACULATE CONCEPTION
(December 8)

ASSUMPTION OF MARY
(August 15)

CHRISTMAS
(December 25)

THE LITURGICAL YEAR

"Christ's saving work is celebrated in sacred memory by the Church on fixed days throughout the year. Each week on the day called the Lord's Day the Church commemorates the Lord's resurrection. Once a year at Easter the Church honors this resurrection and passion with the utmost solemnity. In fact through the yearly cycle the Church unfolds the entire mystery of Christ and keeps the anniversaries of the saints" (General Norms for the Liturgical Year and the Calendar, 1).

The liturgy makes every day of our lives holy, especially when we celebrate the Eucharist and pray the divine office. We celebrate Sunday first of all, because Sunday is the day of the Lord's resurrection.

THE EASTER TRIDUUM

The three days of the Easter Triduum are the most important days of the entire liturgical year; during these days we celebrate the passion and resurrection of Jesus. The Easter Triduum begins with the evening Mass of the Lord's Supper on Holy Thursday. Its high point is the Easter Vigil. The Triduum ends with evening prayer on Easter Sunday.

The Easter Vigil celebrates the "blessed night" when Christ rose from the dead. The Church keeps watch as it awaits Christ's resurrection and welcomes new members of the body of Christ. The entire celebration of this vigil must take place at night.

THE EASTER SEASON

The fifty days from Easter Sunday to Pentecost are celebrated as one "great Sunday." These are the days we sing *Alleluia* and rejoice in our salvation.

THE SEASON OF LENT

During Lent we prepare to celebrate Easter. The liturgy of Lent reminds us of our Baptism. Catechumens prepare for the sacraments of initiation. All Catholics are urged to pray, fast, give alms, and do acts of penance.

THE SEASON OF ADVENT

The liturgical year begins with the first Sunday of Advent. Advent is a time of preparation for Christmas and for Christ's second coming at the end of time. We recall the long years of waiting by the people of Israel for the Messiah, and the faithfulness of Mary and Joseph to God's plan.

THE SEASON OF CHRISTMAS

Christmas is our celebration of Jesus' birth. It begins at the Vigil Mass on Christmas Eve and ends on the feast of the Baptism of the Lord. The season includes the events from Jesus' birth to the beginning of his public ministry.

ORDINARY TIME

Ordinary Time in the Church's year occurs between the Christmas and Lenten seasons, and after the Easter Season until the beginning of Advent. Ordinary Time is devoted to the mystery of Christ in all its aspects.

In this yearly cycle, we also venerate with a special love Mary, the Mother of God. We celebrate the memory of the martyrs and other saints. On Saturdays in Ordinary Time, if there is no obligatory memorial to a saint, a memorial of the Blessed Virgin Mary may be celebrated.

The liturgical year ends with the solemnity of Christ the King, the last Sunday in Ordinary Time.

Index

Italicized numbers refer to definitions   **Bold-faced** numbers refer to chapters

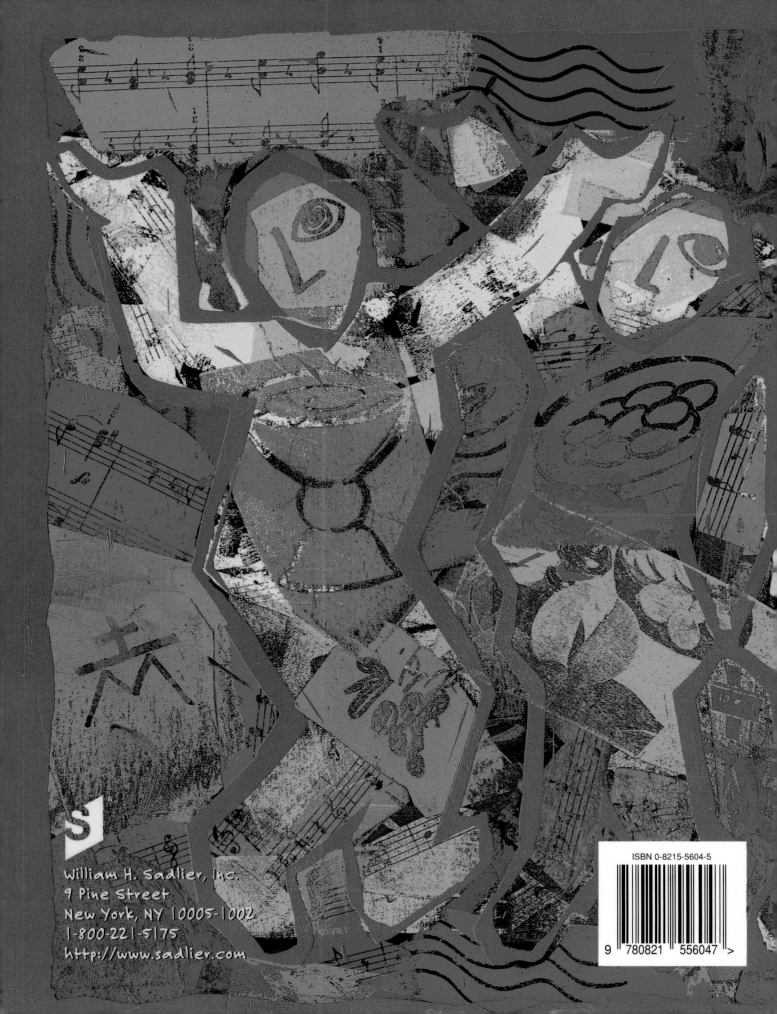

William H. Sadlier, Inc.
9 Pine Street
New York, NY 10005-1002
1-800-221-5175
http://www.sadlier.com

ISBN 0-8215-5604-5

9 780821 556047 >

SOS PLANET EARTH

$3.95 U.S.
$4.95 CAN.

3

12C

NATURE IN DANGER

Troll Associates